"As a cold-case detective, I've seen how unnoticed influences can quietly redirect our lives, sometimes for the better, but often for the worse. Today's technologies are some of the most powerful unseen forces in human history. *Stewarding AI: Faithfully Using Creation Resources* will challenge you to ask not just what your devices and AI tools help you accomplish but what they are doing to your attention, your relationships, your spiritual life, and your character. For Christians who want to guard their hearts and habits while wisely engaging a digital world, this is an essential and timely guide."

—J. Warner Wallace, *Dateline* featured Cold-Case Detective

"This is an important, excellent guide to AI, its promise and perils, from a Christian perspective. The writing is clear, accessible, and persuasive. Highly recommended to anyone interested in assessing the power of AI."

—Charles Taliaferro, Emeritus Overby Distinguished Professor, St. Olaf College

"We find ourselves in a world where AI touches nearly every aspect of our lives—whether we like it or not. Few of us know how to successfully traverse this new landscape, let alone live Christianly in it. The author team of *Stewarding AI* neither condemns AI technology nor uncritically embraces it. Instead, they offer a pathway forward. Using sound biblical principles, they present a framework to guide Christians' use of AI to glorify God and benefit humanity. This thoughtful and accessible work is a must read for Christians and non-Christians alike."

—Fazale "Fuz" Rana, President and CEO, Reasons to Believe

"In the rapidly advancing world of AI that's reshaping how we think, create, and connect, *Stewarding AI* steps in with clear-headed, biblically rooted wisdom that Christians desperately need right now. Deanna Huff, Brian Chilton, and the contributors don't shy away from the real challenges—whether it's the philosophical pitfalls of naturalism, the ethical risks of merging tech with humanity, or the subtle ways chatbots and social media erode true community—but they equip us to engage faithfully. Grounded in Scripture, this book reminds us that technology is a tool for stewardship, not a replacement for human dignity or dependence on God. It's thoughtful, practical, and urgent. Christians, get this book now. The church must grapple with these issues, and this is the resource we need to guide us."

—Brett Kunkle, Founder and President, MAVEN

"I remember being in a major bookstore on the last day of 1999 and seeing Y2K books displayed at a 90 percent discount. You don't need to be a bookstore owner to know that technology books quickly become obsolete. We're glad to say that is not the case with this book. *Stewarding AI* equips Christians with renewed minds to exercise discernment in the use and stewardship of AI and technology as a whole. This book will remain relevant for the questions it asks, the wisdom it draws upon, and the tools it utilizes come from God's timeless word. As a pastor (Jason) and Christian writer (Bev), we are pleased to recommend *Stewarding AI* to Christians looking for clarity in the chaos. Highly recommended!"

—Jason Berrus, Lead Pastor, Immanuel Church, Fullerton, and Beverly Chao Berrus, contributor to *Strong in the Lord: A 30-Day Devotional on the Armor of God*

Stewarding AI

Stewarding AI

Faithfully Using Creation Resources

EDITED BY
DEANNA HUFF
BRIAN G. CHILTON

WIPF & STOCK · Eugene, Oregon

STEWARDING AI
Faithfully Using Creation Resources

Wipf & Stock
An Imprint of Wipf and Stock Publishers
199 W. 8th Ave., Suite 3
Eugene, OR 97401

www.wipfandstock.com

PAPERBACK ISBN: 979-8-3852-7589-2
HARDCOVER ISBN: 979-8-3852-7590-8
EBOOK ISBN: 979-8-3852-7591-5

VERSION NUMBER 04/20/26

For my husband Jimmy, my greatest encourager and example of Christ, and to my kids, Lily, Ellie, and Ranly, who sharpen me and bring me infinite joy. Isaiah 52:7.
—Deanna

To my wife, Jennifer, inquisitive son, Grayson, and to Dr. Michelle Johnson, a colleague who began this journey with us but, due to her untimely passing, is now enjoying an even greater reward in heaven.
—Brian

Deanna and Brian would both like to thank Ryan Pauly and Eric Hernandez, who added a tremendous amount of depth to the book. We are thankful for you both.

Contents

About the Authors

Dr. Deanna Huff is a Christian apologist, author, and speaker based in Oklahoma City. She coauthored *Why Creationism Still Matters* and *Strong Faith*. She is the executive vice president for Bellator Christi and hosts the *Encouraging and Equipping Podcast*. Deanna earned her PhD in theology and apologetics at Liberty University with her dissertation "The Prophets' Use of the Shepherd Motif and Its Contribution to Their Presentation of the Character of God." She holds a ThM in apologetics and worldview from Southern Baptist Theological Seminary, a MDiv with biblical languages from Southwestern Baptist Theological Seminary, and a bachelor of arts from the University of Oklahoma. Boomer Sooner!

Dr. Brian G. Chilton is the founder of Bellator Christi Ministries. He serves as a hospice chaplain and as an assistant director of family services, an adjunct professor of apologetics at Carolina College of Biblical Studies, a dissertation mentor/adjunct professor for Liberty University in the PhD applied apologetics program, and an adjunct professor/dissertation reader at Carolina University in the DMin program. His previous books include *The Layman's Manual on Christian Apologetics*, *Conversations About Heaven*, *Why Creationism Still Matters*, and *Semitic Residue: Signs of Early Oral Traditions in the Gospel of Matthew*. Dr. Chilton holds a PhD in Theology and Apologetics from Liberty University. His research interests are in early Christianity, early Christian oral traditions and creeds, and near-death experiences.

Ryan Pauly is the founder and president of Think Well, the director of immersive experiences at MAVEN, and an adjunct professor of theology and apologetics at Talbot School of Theology, Biola University. He contributed the article "Why Does God Send Good People to Hell?" for the popular

Apologetics Study Bible for Students. Ryan holds a BA in theology and youth leadership from Vanguard University, an MA in Christian apologetics from Biola University, and is a doctoral candidate in practical theology at Talbot School of Theology. Ryan is a Coloradoan at heart but currently resides in Southern California with his wife and three sons. He enjoys watching Colorado Avalanche hockey, roasting coffee, and spending time with his family.

ERIC HERNANDEZ is a Christian apologist, author, and speaker specializing in the philosophy of mind, evangelism, and the rational defense of Christianity. He is the author of *The Lazy Approach to Evangelism: A Simple Guide for Conversing with Nonbelievers* and is featured in the apologetics documentary *Universe Designed*. He formerly served as the apologetics lead and millennial specialist for Texas Baptists. He participated in numerous public debates and dialogues with nonbelievers in academic and ecclesial contexts globally. He serves as a field guide for MAVEN. He holds degrees in theology, Christian ministries, and philosophy as well as a certificate in Christian apologetics from Biola University. Eric is the founder and president of EHM Apologetics, which equips believers to defend the Christian faith.

Introduction

Welcome to the Age of AI

Deanna Huff, PhD

The most authentic wielder of innovation is the one who wields that innovation to love God and love others. Tech is a divine gift to test our stewardship.

—Tony Reinke[1]

The arrival of OpenAI ChatGPT-3 in 2022 became a watershed moment for Artificial Intelligence (AI). In 2025, ChatGPT-5 launched, further changing the landscape of the AI world, ushering in endless opportunities and ethical dilemmas. But AI is not new. So, what changed? Prior to ChatGPT-3, AI was implemented through virtual assistant devices like Alexa and Siri, which used commands and algorithms. It was used in smartphones' face recognition and mapping; emails utilized programs that applied AI spam filters; AI computer applications translated languages; and TV streaming platforms recommended movies for you based on your previous selections, but ChatGPT-3 moved beyond simply filtering algorithms. It generated content, becoming known as Generative AI. Tristan Harris, an American technology ethicist, cautions that while AI can be used for good, we must use this technology responsibly and understand the risks of using AI machines.[2] ChatGPT is a chatbot, and since its arrival, many others have emerged, such as Copilot, Gemini, Claude, and Grok. Chatbots can remember past conversations, interact with new discussions, create recipes, produce music, craft exams, develop PowerPoints, and so much more.

1. Reinke, *God, Technology, and Christian Life*, 301.
2. Harris and Raskin, "AI Dilemma."

While testing Copilot, I requested that it create a song about the fall season, and in under five minutes, it had written a song, an art poster, and a sound file. What does all this mean for humanity? How will people interact with computers? Computer scientists have created a computer that generates so many things for people, and now we must learn to steward it.

When OpenAI released ChatGPT-3, the media quickly broadened AI awareness, resulting in everyday conversations regarding AI's future hopes and fears. Definitions for AI began to expand. The VET artificial Intelligence Act of 2025 defines AI as "a machine-based system that, for explicit or implicit objectives, infers, from the input it receives, how to generate outputs such as predictions, content, recommendations, or decisions that can influence physical or virtual environments. Different AI systems vary in their levels of autonomy and adaptiveness after deployment."[3]

Today, AI is a topic of discussion across almost every discipline, including education, science, business, law, theology, philosophy, history, etc. When speaking with educators, teachers, and professors, they fear that students are allowing computers to do their thinking and writing, resulting in a lack of critical thinking. Yet, when discussing the subject in the business world, I hear leaders express excitement about attempting to maximize time and efficiency by using AI. In the field of science, I hear people discuss advancements in smart devices that automatically shut off the lights and lock the doors, which assist people with disabilities. Others are discussing biomedical technologies that restore health. Some conversations about law involve the rights of producers of music, art, and other creative works. Government meetings on Capitol Hill are addressing the positive and negative effects while attempting to discuss regulations amid many AI-tracking concerns. The reality is that AI has advantages and disadvantages. However, people are having difficulty discussing matters because technology is advancing at an exponential rate. In addition, fear of technology sometimes causes people to dismiss it altogether. Let's not throw out the baby with the bath water. Instead, let's learn to think Christianly about how to steward AI.

This book offers conversation starters that can be applied across various disciplines of AI, equipping Christians with connections to encourage the church to steward AI faithfully and responsibly.

Why can't people ignore AI? Because it is everywhere. Frequently, it goes unnoticed because the transition to using it is natural and benefits society. In 2023, Forbes highlighted the benefits of AI in healthcare through

3. Hickenlooper, "VET Artificial Intelligence Act," 2–3.

the use of monitoring devices. *Forbes* author and world-renowned futurist Bernard Marr wrote,

> AI has also made a substantial impact on healthcare through the integration of wearable devices and IoT-enabled health monitoring systems, which are devices connected to the internet. These technologies continuously collect valuable patient data like heart rate, blood pressure, and glucose levels, so healthcare providers can monitor and manage chronic conditions more effectively.[4]

In education, Marr writes, "AI-driven language translation tools and real-time transcription services have broken down language barriers, enabling students worldwide to access educational content from anywhere in the world."[5] The list of benefits will be further explored in the following chapters, along with some of the drawbacks that should be thoughtfully considered.

AI users should be aware of the unintended consequences that produce adverse outcomes. For example, social media offers the benefits of connecting with family and friends, giving people a voice, and providing advertising opportunities for businesses. However, negative effects have been identified through mental health issues, bullying, lack of attention spans, phone addictions, information overload, disinformation, and censorship. The new neurotechnology is raising concerns over privacy acts and expectations in the workplace. Nita Farahany sounded the alarm in her book *The Battle for the Brain*, revealing the possible overreach of sharing brain sensor information without individual consent. The research in the following chapters will reveal some of these potential risks that should stimulate us to consider in our AI conversations.

In the book *The Age of AI*, Jason Thacker posed two questions when engaging in AI conversations: What is it to be human, and what is AI?[6] Rightly, he believes biblical principles should answer these questions and guide people when navigating AI decisions. Thacker writes that AI "is not good or evil in itself but can be designed and used for good and evil purposes. We can use technology for the glory of God and the betterment of society, or we can use it to push aside the dignity of others created in God's image for sinful and contorted means."[7]

4. Marr, "15 Amazing Real-World Applications," para. 4.
5. Marr, "15 Amazing Real-World Applications," para. 22.
6. Thacker, *Age of AI*, 16.
7. Thacker, *Age of AI*, 26.

It is essential to recognize that God's word offers principles to navigate the conversations of AI and guide us in how we steward AI. First, we should utilize technology in a way that reflects our love for God and our love for our neighbor. Second, it is essential to recognize that humans are created in God's image. Third, incorporating AI should entail biblical stewardship. God appointed man to steward and care for the world. Stewardship is the responsible care for something that has been entrusted to you. Since God is the Creator of all things, all things belong to him (Gen 1:1). While he created all things, he has delegated the care of the world to humanity. He has allowed people to discover many things in the world, and the way we use all things should bring glory to him. God is the owner, and we are the managers. This book will focus on the stewardship extended to humanity by God, as described in the beginning pages of the Bible, which will sustain the claim that Christians should give careful thought and be good stewards of AI.

CHECKPOINTS BEFORE MOVING FORWARD

The authors of this book seek to stimulate theological and technological discussions with Christians and non-Christians. While the book's content is geared toward Christians, we believe that the principles are universal. There are many experts in the field of AI, but we should all consider the impact of AI on our lives. John Lennox says, "It is clear that one does not need to know how to build an autonomous vehicle or weapon in order to have an informed view about the ethics of deploying such things. You don't need to know how to program an AI tracker system in order to have a valid opinion about invasion of privacy."[8] The church needs leaders to engage in the intersection of theology and technology. We need to consider the advantages, disadvantages, limitations, and unintended consequences. We need to discuss theological, philosophical, and ethical issues. All of these conversations should be in light of Scripture and prepare us to interact with the world of AI. This book is too brief to be exhaustive; rather, it serves as a springboard to start the AI conversations. Christians have the opportunity to lead the conversation. We can start by asking a few questions. The following questions can promote AI conversations, yet they are far from exhaustive:

8. Lennox, *2084*, 10.

What Are Biblical Principles to Use Regarding AI?

The biblical principles of loving God and loving our neighbor as ourselves should guide our discernment in making AI decisions, as this is the example Christ delivered in Matt 22:36–40:[9]

> A lawyer, asked Him a question, testing Him, "Teacher, which is the great commandment in the Law?" And He said to him, "'You shall love the Lord your God with all your heart, and with all your soul, and with all your mind.' This is the great and foremost commandment. The second is like it, 'You shall love your neighbor as yourself.' On these two commandments depend the whole Law and the Prophets."

When encountering technology, people should ask if this technology reflects love for God and love for others.

Are Christians Stewarding Technology, or Is Technology Stewarding Christians?

Genesis 1:28–31 states,

> God created man in His own image, in the image of God He created him; male and female He created them. God blessed them; and God said to them, "Be fruitful and multiply, and fill the earth, and subdue it; and rule over the fish of the sea and over the birds of the sky and over every living thing that moves on the earth." Then God said, "Behold, I have given you every plant yielding seed that is on the surface of all the earth, and every tree which has fruit yielding seed; it shall be food for you; and to every beast of the earth and to every bird of the sky and to everything that moves on the earth which has life, I have given every green plant for food"; and it was so. God saw all that He had made, and behold, it was very good.

God created all things and delegated authority to people to rule and utilize the resources. How is it going?

9. Unless otherwise noted, all Scripture quoted in this introduction is taken from the Christian Standard Bible (NASB).

How Does the Fall of Man Impact the Decision-Making Process?

In the beginning, humanity was created perfect, but due to humanity's disobedience to God, humanity was separated from God and desires to uphold their own ways. But when people trust in Christ, they receive the Holy Spirit, which enables them to discern between the things of God and worldly thinking if they are putting on the mind of Christ. Although man is not perfect, the Holy Spirit will guide his discernment. John 16:13–15 says,

> But when He, the Spirit of truth, comes, He will guide you into all the truth; for He will not speak on His own initiative, but whatever He hears, He will speak; and He will disclose to you what is to come. He will glorify Me, for He will take of Mine and will disclose it to you. All things that the Father has are Mine; therefore I said that He takes of Mine and will disclose it to you.

Christians have the Holy Spirit, which will guide them in pursuing wisdom if they seek God in the use of technology.

Are Machines Being Humanized, and Are People Being Dehumanized?

God's word says that people have value because humanity is made in the image of God. Genesis 1:27a states, "Then God said, 'Let Us make man in Our image, according to Our likeness.'" However, news articles are warning that machines and technology are shaping how people think and value one another. Are humans expressing value for humanity in the process of using these technologies? In using technology, there must be an awareness and thoughtful conversations regarding these issues.

Is This Technology Causing People to Flourish?

Discovering the resources in God's creation is an exciting and useful endeavor. The discovery of light, air conditioning, and many other discoveries have flourished societies for the good. Christians who seek to lessen the pain and suffering of others are doing commendable work, but we should be thoughtful about these advancements. Unintended consequences often go unnoticed until the costs are greater than expected.

When heading into new AI territory, it is a benefit to think about checkpoints that would benefit the whole of society. These checkpoints can start with the previous five questions and then proceed to explore more. The following chapters will expand the discussion on the ideas Christians should consider:

1. Stewardship is God's delegation to man to rule and use creation's resources to flourish in society.
2. Stewardship is using God's wisdom.
3. Stewarding AI should glorify God.

IN THIS BOOK

The following chapters will equip Christians and non-Christians with tools to evaluate the benefits and threats of AI in various ways. The book will provide wisdom in navigating how to decline, decrease, increase, or advance technologies. The reader will be guided in thoughtful conversations about AI that encourage godly stewardship of today's technology. Chapter 1 will explore the philosophy of the way we think and talk about AI, presented by Eric Hernandez and Ryan Pauly. Chapter 2 will discuss AI and human flourishing with Ryan Pauly. Chapter 3 will examine the pros and cons of ChatGPT and plagiarism for people with Dr. Brian Chilton. Chapter 4 will take a closer look at the dangers of brain sensors with Dr. Brian Chilton. In Chapter 5, I will discuss the merging of technology with humanity and refute transhumanism. In Chapter 6, I will focus on social media, chatbots, and community. The conclusion will remind readers that God's wisdom is universal and benefits all of society. Let's get started in developing conversation starters and tips for stewarding AI.

BIBLIOGRAPHY

Harris, Tristan, and Aza Raskin. "The A.I. Dilemma—March 9, 2023." Center for Humane Technology, Apr. 5, 2023. YouTube video, 1:01:30. https://www.youtube.com/watch?v=xoVJKj8lcNQ.

Hickenlooper, John W. "VET Artificial Intelligence Act." S. Res. S.2615, 119th Congress (2025–2026), July 31, 2025. https://www.congress.gov/bill/119th-congress/senate-bill/2615/text.

Lennox, John C. *2084: Artificial Intelligence and the Future of Humanity*. Grand Rapids: Zondervan Reflective, 2020.

Marr, Bernard. "15 Amazing Real-World Applications Of AI Everyone Should Know About." *Forbes*, May 12, 2023. https://www.forbes.com/sites/bernardmarr/2023/05/10/15-amazing-real-world-applications-of-ai-everyone-should-know-about/.

Reinke, Tony. *God, Technology, and the Christian Life.* Wheaton, IL: Crossway, 2022.

Thacker, Jason. *The Age of AI: Artificial Intelligence and the Future of Humanity.* Grand Rapids: Zondervan, 2020.

1

Stewarding the Way We Think and Talk About AI

Eric Hernandez and Ryan Pauly

"Can you do me a favor and point to what part of your body thinks?" I (Eric) asked the congregation.[1] Without hesitation, virtually everyone pointed to their head. "Brain?" I asked for clarification. "Do you need a brain to think?" They nodded their heads yes. "I see. So, does God have a brain?" At this point, most refrained from answering or gazed in confusion as if the thought had never crossed their mind. What's worse is that some responded by saying, "Yes, God has a brain!"

After glancing at the church's sign to confirm I'm not in a Mormon church (Mormons believe that God has a physical body), I explain that the answer is no, God does *not* have a brain. As Scripture teaches, "God is spirit, and those who worship him must worship in spirit and in truth" (John 4:24 ESV). But does God think? Undoubtedly, yes, and Scripture states his thoughts are more than the grains of sand (Ps 139:17–18). But now it seems we have a conundrum on our hands.

If the brain is what thinks and is necessary for it, then how is it that God has no brain and yet thinks just fine? Moreover, are we not made in his image, and if so, why do we assume it's our physical brains that do the

1. Hernandez, *Lazy Approach to Evangelism*, 100.

thinking? Put differently, why do most Christians find themselves in this conundrum after being presented with these questions? Because, quite frankly, this never should've been a conundrum to begin with. Throughout the history of Christianity, the church has always held to the doctrine of a soul that grounds one's faculty of mind, both of which are immaterial, non-physical entities. So, if I may come clean, my first question (What part of your body thinks?) was a trick question. Because, see, if we are made in God's image—immaterial souls with minds—then there is no part of your body that "thinks." Your mind does, and your mind isn't physical. But sadly, most Christians think like naturalists without even realizing it. And this is the underlying problem that I want to address—the way we think and talk about the mind and, in turn, the way we think and talk about AI.

UNPACKING THE PROBLEM

We live in a culture shaped by worldview assumptions that subtly influence not just how we think but how we speak, often without us realizing it. Over time, these ideas have quietly crept into the church, largely unnoticed and rarely challenged. Thus, our exploration of this issue will be threefold. First, we'll unpack the root cause of the problem that stems from an unbiblical worldview known as naturalism. We'll examine how it views reality, the mind, and its direct opposition to a biblical worldview. From here, we'll turn to a Christian understanding of persons—the nature of the soul and mind—in comparison to naturalism and see why the latter fails.

Finally, we'll look at the implications all this has for the way we *should* think and talk about AI.

Naturalism

For our purposes here, *naturalism* can be defined as the belief that the physical world is all that exists, nothing more, nothing less.[2] From this foundation, two more "isms" are worth unpacking that are associated with (if not inherent) to naturalism as a worldview. The first is *reductionism*—the naturalist's attempt to explain some entity X by reducing it to some

2. See Moreland and Craig, *Philosophical Foundations for Christian Worldview*, 129, 381.

entity Y.[3] This can be identified by spotting the "*nothing but*" or "*nothing more than*" language. For example, if I said that marriage is *nothing but* signing a piece of paper for the government, then I've reduced the essence of marriage to *nothing more than* a legal document. Within naturalism, everything (prayers, miracles, souls, etc.) is reduced and explained away as *nothing more than* physics and chemistry. When applied to human beings, this leads to *physicalism*—the view that human beings are reducible *to nothing more than* physical properties and parts; no soul is needed to explain anything. Now consider how the underlying assumptions of this worldview played out above.

We know that when a person thinks, there is neurological activity in the brain. Because of this, we're told by a naturalized culture that it's the brain that thinks. This is presented as a scientific fact, as if it were a spiritually neutral view. And sadly, much of the church has quietly conceded the point, confining "spiritual" discussions about the soul to Sunday school. Granted, we are immaterial souls made in the image of an immaterial God, but sure, let's agree it's the brain that thinks, not the immaterial mind. No harm, no foul. Yet, this isn't a point of neutrality; it's naturalism!

Nevertheless, if naturalism is true, then of course it makes sense to claim that it's the brain that thinks, given that everything can and must be reduced to the physical, natural world. Hence, physicalism via reductionism. And if that's true of the brain, why not of AI? If minds are nothing more than physical processes, then a physical machine like AI could, in principle, be conscious. But that's precisely where this conflicts with a Christian worldview, and at this point, its opposition should be obvious. If the natural world is all that exists, then a God who is, by definition, supernatural (literally, beyond nature) cannot exist. Additionally, Scripture tells us in 1 Cor 15 that if there is no resurrection, then our faith is in vain, and Christianity is false.

By the same token, if there is no soul, there can be no resurrection, and thus, Christianity is false.

This raises an uncomfortable but profoundly important question: Should Christians really be believing (or even assuming) that the brain (or any other physical thing) thinks? Are we not, perhaps unknowingly, reinforcing naturalistic assumptions that undermine the very foundations of our faith, making our worldview seem less plausible to a culture that's already hostile to it? Because, as explained above, not only does this way of

3. Moreland and Rae, *Body and Soul*, 64, 290.

thinking contradict the nature of God, but, given that we're made in his image, it also contradicts the Christian understanding concerning the nature of the mind and soul as well. Thus, the underlying problem. And this is why the way we think and speak about AI matters.

Distinguished Baylor University professor Alan Jacobs wrote about this exact issue in his book *How To Think*. In his section on the power of myth, he writes, "We use metaphors without knowing that they are metaphors. . . . The myths we choose, or more likely simply inherit, do a tremendous amount of intellectual heavy lifting for us."[4] This is exactly why our thinking about AI matters so much. Without critical reflection, the quick adoption of metaphors like "The brain is like a computer" can quickly change our thinking to "The brain is a computer." Yet, as Jacobs continues, "Despite what thousands of computer scientists, neuroscientists, and philosophers will tell you, the human brain is not a computer."[5] This type of uncritical thinking fails to account for the mind and leads to a false understanding of the brain and thoughts.

Yet, because the church has failed to think holistically about worldview issues, we've absorbed these naturalistic ideas without question, assuming they're harmless and separate from "spiritual matters." Hence, we engage in their language—talking about a "brain that thinks"—then walk into church Sunday morning and worship a God that has no brain and thinks just fine, but we never let these two contradictory beliefs meet. Why? Because, again, we haven't learned (or been trained) to think holistically about these issues as they relate to worldview. Put differently, it's not that we've failed to think but that we've failed to think about our thinking, not that we've failed to form beliefs but have failed to biblically form beliefs about our beliefs. We lack holistic worldview thinking. Hence, there was no implicit conundrum in my introductory question above, just an implicit conundrum in how we un-holistically think about these issues. Nevertheless, if a naturalist view concerning the nature of the mind is false, then what view of persons should Christians affirm and defend instead? That's where we now turn.

4. More specifically, "strict physicalism." Moreland and Rae, *Body and Soul*, 93.

5. Jacobs, *How to Think*, 103.

A Christian View of Persons: The Nature of the Soul and Mind

According to historic Christianity, human beings are not physical bodies that "have" souls.[6] Rather, we are immaterial souls who have bodies. The soul, classically understood, is an immaterial substance that possesses consciousness and animates the body.[7] This is a biblical perspective known as *substance dualism*, which teaches that the soul is the essential self, while the body is something the soul inhabits. Put differently, on this view, I don't "have" a soul, but rather, I *am* a soul that *has* a body, and without the soul, a body is nothing more than a corpse. Yet, under the growing influence of naturalism, this understanding has been steadily pushed aside. Today, many accept the idea that human beings are *nothing more than* physical brains and bodies (i.e., physicalism) and assume that the belief in an immaterial soul is simply an outdated, religious belief based upon scientific ignorance.[8]

WHY NATURALISM FAILS

When it comes to the question of the soul, the first thing to be said here is that science is both incompetent and irrelevant for answering the question.[9] Why? Because the soul, if it exists, is by definition a non-physical entity, whereas science, though a wonderful tool for studying the physical world, is a tool that is limited to *only* studying the physical world. Thus, one cannot demand that a discipline like science—which is limited to the physical—must be used to investigate something non-physical. To do so would be like asking me to use a ruler to measure my weight. It's simply the wrong tool for the assessment.

Second, note that if physicalism (via naturalism) is true, then the mind must be *identical* and/or *reducible* to something physical like the brain.[10] This is a claim of identity. In philosophy, when we say that X is *identical* to Y, we simply mean that X is literally *the same thing as* Y. For example, suppose I said that Eric Hernandez is *identical* to the person writing this paragraph. In this case, I'm referring to one person, not two, because Eric

6. Cooper, *Body, Soul, and Life Everlasting*, 31, 33.

7. Moreland and Craig, *Philosophical Foundations for Christian Worldview*, 254–55, 265–67, 325.

8. Rickabaugh and Moreland, *Substance of Consciousness*, 4.

9. In philosophy, this commits what is known as a category fallacy.

10. Moreland and Craig, *Philosophical Foundations for Christian Worldview*, 212.

Hernandez and the person writing this paragraph are the *same* person. Hence, I'm using two labels to refer to *one thing*. As a test for identity, this is known as Leibniz's law of identity, but for brevity's sake, we'll simply refer to this as Leibniz's law.

According to Leibniz's law, if two things in question are identical, say, some X and Y, then whatever is true of X will *necessarily* be true of Y (and vice versa). However, if we can find just *one thing* true of X that is not true of Y (or vice versa), then they cannot be the same thing (i.e., they cannot be identical). To illustrate, imagine you're in a lab looking at two bottles of clear fluids. One bottle is labeled "water," and the other is "chemical X," but suppose that the label for one was worn out and illegible.

Applying Leibniz's law, you want to know if these are the same substance because, as far as you can tell, they are identical. Both are fluids, both are transparent, and thus, you assume they must be the same substance. But then you turn over the bottle of chemical X and find a warning label that reads, "Caution: Flammable." Given that water is not flammable, but chemical X is, you now conclude that, contrary to your initial assumption, *the two cannot be the same substance*. Therefore, even if you don't know what chemical X is, you now know that, given Leibniz's law, they cannot be *identical*.

Now apply this to physicalism. If your mind really is identical and reducible to your brain, then everything true of your mind must also be true of your brain and vice versa. However, this would also mean that if we can find *just one thing* true of the mind that's not true of the brain (or vice versa), then, given Leibniz's law, they cannot be the same thing. And this is where physicalism (or any view that grounds the mind in something physical) collapses and is precisely why the existence and nature of consciousness becomes a problem for the naturalist.

Cause-Effect and Dependency—Identity or Mere Correlation?

In defense of physicalism, many naturalists point to the cause-effect or dependency relationship between the mind and brain. After all, we know from neuroscience that when a mental state occurs (e.g., a thought or belief), there will be a correlating brain state (i.e., neurons firing). Furthermore, we know that in cases of brain damage (such as Alzheimer's), certain regions of the brain are directly correlated with certain functions of the mind (such as memory).

As a result, damage to these regions has a direct effect on one's functional ability to recall memories. This suffices to demonstrate two things:

1. a *cause-and-effect relationship* between the mind and brain, and
2. a *dependence relationship* between specified regions of the brain and specified functions of the mind.

From these observations, the naturalist concludes that the mind and brain must therefore be the same thing. But is that conclusion justified? Has neuroscience settled the matter and buried the Christian worldview? No, and for one simple reason: *cause and effect or dependency does not establish identity.*[11]

To illustrate why this popular argument fails, consider the relationship between a musician and his instrument. A guitarist knows that to successfully play the note C, he must first press down and strum a specific group of correlated strings. Similarly, he knows that if these correlating strings were to pop, he could no longer play the note. As before, this suffices to establish two things:

1. a *cause-and-effect relationship* between the guitarist and his guitar, and
2. a *dependence relationship* between specified regions of the guitar for specified functions of the notes.

But what follows from this? Nothing important or profound.

No one would say that because a guitarist depends on his guitar, therefore, he is identical to his guitar, or that the note C and its correlated strings are reducible to one another. Similarly, just as detuning a guitar (which affects the pitch and sound of the music) doesn't prove that the note C is *identical, reducible,* or *located within* a physical region of the guitar, showing a correlation between my mind and brain doesn't prove that my thoughts are *identical, reducible,* or *located within* the physical regions of my brain. This is because, once again, *establishing a cause-effect or dependency relation does not establish identity.*

11. Moreland and Rae, *Body and Soul*, 58; Moreland and Craig, *Philosophical Foundations for Christian Worldview*, 213.

The Non-Identity of Mind and Matter

To reiterate, if physicalism is true, then the mind must be *reducible* and/or *identical* to something physical like the brain. However, if we can demonstrate the *non-identity* of mind and matter (or, in this case, mind and brain), then given Leibniz's law, it would follow that physicalism is false and thus cannot account for the nature of human beings (i.e., an immaterial soul that grounds an immaterial mind). Unfortunately for the physicalist, this is trivially easy to do, and mind you, we only need *one example*. Using Leibniz's law, here are three points in defense of dualism demonstrating that the mind and brain are *not* the same thing.

1. *A belief is a mental state that can be true or false, but no state or region of my brain can be true or false.* Therefore, if a belief can be true or false, but its correlating neurons cannot, then the mind and brain cannot be the same thing.
2. *My brain can weigh three pounds, but my thought that grass is green does not weigh three pounds.* While you may have "heavy thoughts" reading this chapter, it will not require a neck brace. Hence, if my brain possesses weight, but my thoughts do not, then they cannot be the same thing.
3. *My brain can be in a state that measures seven inches long, but the smell of a rose or the taste of a banana (which are states of my mind) is not seven inches long.* Sensory experiences don't occupy physical space; brain tissue does. Therefore, if my brain can have a length but my mental states do not, they cannot be the same thing.

Consequently, if all the states and properties of my brain are physical, but all the states and properties of my mind are not physical, then it follows that if consciousness exists, it is neither reducible nor identical to anything physical like the brain. However, if consciousness exists and cannot be physical, then, consequently, physicalism cannot be true. In a syllogism, this argument can be written as follows:

1. If physicalism is true, then consciousness must be physical.
2. Consciousness is not physical.
3. Therefore, physicalism is false.

Having exposed the failure of naturalism and its physicalist view of human beings, what does this mean for AI? Simply this: if the brain doesn't think, then machines never will. Why? Because if it's the immaterial soul that grounds the mind, then no purely physical thing, no matter how advanced, can think. This realization reframes the entire conversation and raises an important question: How should we, as believers, think and talk about AI within a Christian worldview?

THINKING AND TALKING ABOUT AI WITHIN A CHRISTIAN WORLDVIEW

With the rapid development of "artificial intelligence," many are beginning to seriously ask—will AI ever become conscious? As we've seen, the short answer is no. But before expanding on the reasons, consider the implications. If consciousness requires a soul, then anything with a mind must also "possess" a soul. This leads to an unsettling hypothetical: if AI were ever to become conscious, that would imply AI has a *soul*, since, as we've established, purely physical entities cannot ground immaterial consciousness. If that were true, where would it leave us? Would we be morally obligated to treat AI as persons? Would insulting or mistreating a chatbot be sinful? And if an AI were a person, would it, too, be made in God's image? If so, would we need to evangelize every AI bot out there? Could an AI bot sin? Could it be held morally accountable? The implications behind this are endless. However, note how this entire discussion hinges on a faulty assumption: that AI could become conscious. It can't—and understanding why will clarify how Christians should frame the issue.

Machines Are Material; the Mind Is Not

If your brain (a living organ designed by God) cannot account for your mind, then surely no artificial machine, regardless of its complexity, can either. Granted, AI may *function* as if it were conscious, but this cannot establish that the states of my mind and the functions of AI are identical. As before, my thoughts can be true or false, but functions cannot be true or false. After all, my engine running is a function, but engines do not run "true" or "false." Hence, the two cannot be the same thing.[12]

12. Moreland and Rae, *Body and Soul*, 157–60.

When we look at the world around us, we can see that there is something inherently different about humans. Machines may be able to lift more, jump higher, or run faster, but that doesn't mean that machines are the same as humans. Professor Lennox puts it this way: "It is one thing to make a machine that can simulate, say, a human hand lifting an object; it is a completely different thing to make a machine that can simulate the thoughts of a human when he or she is lifting an object."[13] The reason for the unlikelihood of a general AI (a system that can do all that human intelligence can do) ever being developed is that humans have something that machines will never have: a mind. Machines will get better at simulating our thoughts but will never be able to truly think. When Mustafa Suleyman, a leading AI researcher and cofounder of DeepMind, asks whether we can distill the essence of humans into an algorithm, he assumes that we are purely physical beings. As we hope you see in this chapter, this is not the case.

Thoughts Are Immaterial; AI Is Not

Consciousness, as we've established, is immaterial. It cannot be *reduced to* or *located within* anything physical. To illustrate this point, consider something philosophers call *first-person private access.*[14] While a neuroscientist might know more about my brain than I do, she will never know more about my thoughts than I do. Why? Because only I have privileged, private access to my thoughts. My mind is private. My brain is not. You can open my skull and study my brain, but you can't open my skull and see my thoughts.

Now contrast this with AI. A machine's code and functions are fully accessible to any technician with the right tools. There's no hidden, first-person experience inside a machine, only lines of code and mechanical processes producing outputs. AI has no private, inner world—no privileged access to its own "thoughts," because there are none. Therefore, the mind is privately accessible, but AI functions are externally observable and publicly accessible; the two cannot be the same thing. Lacking this essential feature of consciousness, AI necessarily lacks consciousness itself.

13. Lennox, *2084*, 17.

14. For an introductory treatment on these aspects, see Moreland, *Soul*, 26, 79–80, 92.

Intentionality: The Code vs. the Coder

Another essential feature unique to the mind is known as *intentionality*—the notion that the mind can be "of" or "about" something.[15] For example, when I have a sensation of hunger, there will be a correlated group of neurons firing in my brain. My sensation may be "of" or "about" food, but the correlated firing neurons are not hungry, much less "of" or "about" the food I'm desiring. For example, you think about your day, about what you will eat for lunch, or about the chapter you are currently reading. Your thoughts are always about something. On the contrary, physical objects, from neurons to chairs to phones, are never about anything. They just are. Mental states have "aboutness," whereas physical things have "isness."

To see how AI fails to account for this feature, consider the notion of making a mistake. If a computer tells me that 2+2=5, then, at best, we can call it a glitch, but it wouldn't be appropriate to call it a "mistake." Why not? Because mistakes imply intentionality, which doesn't come from the code but the coder. Therefore, if my mind possesses the essential feature of intentionality, but physical states, processes, or programs do not, then it follows that the two cannot be the same thing. Thus, any notion of intentionality (e.g., a mistake) must be applied to a mind, which is grounded in the programmer, not the program.

Moral Responsibility: Humans Possess Free Will; AI Does Not

To build upon the previous point, consider the notion of free will, which can be defined as being the originator and first mover of one's will or action.[16] This is, in part, what it means to be made in the image of God. Human beings are not merely reacting to prior, external causes; we can initiate actions by choice. By contrast, purely physical objects do not possess this capacity. Their movements and behaviors are entirely determined by prior causes: chemical reactions, physical laws, or external inputs. In short, purely physical objects do not act on their own but are caused to act by prior external forces governed by the laws of chemistry and physics (i.e., the inputs and outputs).

15. Moreland, *Soul*, 80.

16. Moreland and Craig, *Philosophical Foundations for Christian Worldview*, 259–60.

Eric[17] and I both had the opportunity to debate atheist YouTuber Tom Jump. In my discussion, Tom stated, "We can definitely take purely physical things with no consciousness, and they can figure out which is the correct path. Even rocks know the correct path of the shortest distance from falling down a cliff. . . . We know that biology can actually do math."[18] When pressed on the issue, it became clear that his uses of "know" and "figure out" were merely figures of speech. Physical things are determined by prior causes and, as such, do not "know" or "figure things out" like a conscious human being with free will.

Consider a simple example: suppose I program my coffee maker to start brewing at 5:00 a.m. tomorrow. By the time it starts, I'll still be asleep. Nevertheless, even though I'm unconscious when it starts brewing, I am still the responsible agent behind the act. The coffee maker didn't *choose* to start brewing and act on its own but was caused to act by my prior external input. It couldn't have done otherwise. Hence, responsibility must be traced back to the first mover of a chain.[19]

It is for this reason that if a "self-driving" car crashes into another vehicle, we do not blame the car itself. Why not? Because, like intentionality, free will belongs to a mind, not a machine. As before, finding moral blame must be traced back to the first mover. Namely, the designer and programmer of the car. Therefore, if an essential attribute of persons entails moral responsibility, which assumes the free will that AI (being a purely physical machine) lacks, then the two cannot be the same thing (nor can the latter ever be reduced to the former). AI, at its core, is just a sophisticated tool, not a moral agent.

OBJECTIONS

Objection 1: But Mind Emerges from Matter

At this point, a common argument presented in favor of physicalism is the claim that the mind is simply an emergent property of the brain, much like wetness is an emergent property of H_2O. The reasoning goes like this: neither hydrogen nor oxygen, on their own, possesses the property of "wetness." However, when these two elements are combined in the right way to

17. Jump and Hernandez, "Freewill, Consciousness, and Existence."
18. Pauly, "Reasons to Believe in God," 45:51.
19. Moreland and Craig, *Philosophical Foundations for Christian Worldview*, 307–8.

form water, presto! The property of wetness appears. In a similar manner (argues the naturalist), if the brain reaches a certain level of complexity and organization, consciousness emerges. And if that's the case, then in principle, the right physical conditions could also allow a mind (or even a soul) to emerge from sufficiently complex systems like AI.

At first glance, this analogy sounds plausible. But upon closer inspection, the argument collapses, and for several reasons. Let's briefly examine a few. First, the analogy of wetness being an emergent property of H_2O is, at best, an example of rearranging a physical base (hydrogen and oxygen) in order to get a different *physical* property (wetness). But the problem here is obvious: consciousness is not a physical property. If consciousness is immaterial (as we've argued), then the argument from analogy fails to prove anything relevant. Rearranging physical things to get a new physical outcome is categorically different from claiming that rearranging physical things can generate something *fundamentally immaterial* like consciousness.

This leads us to the second problem, which has been argued by atheist philosopher Thomas Nagel. In his book *Mind and Cosmos: Why the Materialist Neo-Darwinian Conception of Nature is Almost Certainly False*, Nagel essentially argues that you cannot get mind from matter.[20] Simply put, if all you do is rearrange matter, then all you will get is more complicated chunks of matter, but you won't get mind popping into existence. The third problem can be seen as an extension of the previous.

The only way to get "new" or different properties of matter is to rearrange what is already there into a new physical structure. In philosophy, these are known as *structural properties*.[21] To illustrate, a stack of red bricks possesses the property of being a pile, and when rearranged into a new configuration, these same base parts can now possess the new *structural*

20. Nagel, *Mind and Cosmos*. Consider the following quotes: "It seems to me that, as it is usually presented, the current orthodoxy about the cosmic order is the product of governing assumptions that are unsupported, and that it flies in the face of common sense" (5). "If the mental is not itself merely physical, it cannot be fully explained by physical science" (14). "Consciousness is the most conspicuous obstacle to a comprehensive naturalism that relies only on the resources of physical science. . . . If we take this problem seriously, and follow out its implications, it threatens to unravel the entire naturalistic world picture" (35). "It would be an advance if the secular theoretical establishment, and the contemporary enlightened culture which it dominates, could wean itself of the materialism and Darwinism of the gaps—to use one of its own pejorative tags. I have tried to show that this approach is incapable of providing an adequate account, either constitutive or historical, of our universe" (127).

21. Moreland and Rae, *Body and Soul*, 101

property of being a house. Thus, structural properties are merely new patterns of the matter that was already there to begin with. However, no amount of addition, subtraction, or rearrangement of these red bricks could ever produce the color blue. Why not? Because blueness is not a structural property (like a house or pile) that can emerge from a new pattern of matter. It's categorically different. And just as the property of blueness cannot emerge from a rearrangement of red bricks, the property of consciousness cannot emerge from a mere rearrangement of matter.

Like blueness, consciousness is not the kind of thing that "emerges" from complex configurations of physical components. When applied to the argument for AI, the same problems follow. No matter how advanced the system, no matter how sophisticated the coding or hardware becomes, it remains purely physical. Again, just as no arrangement of red bricks will yield the property of blueness, no configuration of circuits and algorithms will ever generate consciousness. The attempt to explain the mind as an emergent property from physical processes, whether in brains or in machines, simply fails.

Objection 2: But AI Acts Just Like Us

It is important to note that any argument for the claim that AI could one day become conscious and self-aware like us hinges on a physicalist view of personhood, typically framed within the philosophies of *behaviorism* or *functionalism*. In either model, personhood is reduced to behaviors or functions reacting to certain inputs.[22] Thus, if purely physical machines (e.g., AI computers or robots) function or behave just as we do, then they must be (or will one day become) conscious and self-aware just like us. After all, if consciousness is nothing more than the right set of functions or behaviors, then what difference does it make whether these are performed by neurons or microchips? However, exposing the failure of this model is trivially easy to do.

If I were stuck with a needle and shouted, "Ouch!" it would make sense to assume that I'm in a mental state of pain. However, if I programmed a robot to do the same, it wouldn't follow, therefore, that the robot must be in pain. Why not? Because *imitating* consciousness (i.e., the "right" behaviors or functions) is not the same thing as *possessing* consciousness. After all, even a talented actor could exhibit the "right" inputs and outputs of pain

22. Moreland, *Soul*, 102.

while lacking the conscious sensation. Thus, a sophisticated imitation, no matter how convincing, is still just an imitation.

Even the atheist philosopher John Searle (one of the leading experts within the philosophy of mind) recognized this issue. As a thought experiment, Searle offers a counterexample in what he calls the Chinese Room argument.[23] To summarize the argument, imagine that you are locked in a room with only one slot on the door. In that room, you are given a rule book with instructions explaining that when a person passes in a note with certain squiggly-squiggly symbols, you are to return a note that has certain squiggly-squiggly symbols. But what you aren't told is that the notes being handed in are actually questions in Chinese, and the notes that you are handing back are the corresponding Chinese answers. Now, suppose you become so good at this process that the people on the outside take you to be a fluent Chinese speaker, when in reality, you don't understand a word of Chinese.

The point of Searle's argument is simple: imitating the behaviors of a Chinese speaker doesn't make one fluent in Chinese. Concerning AI robots or computers, the same conclusion follows. Machines operate and are functionally equivalent to the person inside the Chinese room. And just as following a program for imitating Chinese does not make one a fluent Chinese speaker, it equally follows that a computer being programmed to imitate consciousness does not make it a conscious being. AI merely imitates mental functions and behaviors; it does not possess them. Regardless of how human-like its responses may seem, AI remains what it always has been: a machine. Again, no matter how sophisticated or convincing the imitation, it's still just an imitation.

There is currently a branch of modern AI called machine learning, which uses algorithms to analyze data and learn from experiences. Programs like ChatGPT would be an example of these large language models (LLMs). I (Pauly) interviewed Sean Thunquest, a Cloud engineer at Hewlett-Packard, and he described these LLMs as being able to generate responses that sound believable, but they are not designed for understanding. Humans can "create understanding from observations" and break down our problems, understand them, and improvise to create something better.[24] LLMs appear to do this because they can generate responses based on "learned" patterns from analyzing vast amounts of data, and their functions

23. Searle, *Minds, Brains, and Science*, 32–33.

24. Sean Thunquest, e-mail message to author (Ryan Pauly), Aug. 17, 2024.

are what Suleyman calls "black boxes." While research and understanding are growing, the outputs of these LLMs are difficult to trace.[25] At the same time, we know that the outputs are completely determined by the inputs. There is no thought, understanding, or choice being made. As Lennox puts it, "They don't 'crunch' without a human in the loop at some level guiding the whole process. . . . The human involvement is conscious. The machine is not."[26] This is where humans continue to be uniquely different from machines.

THE TAKEAWAY

At the start of this chapter, we explored how failing to recognize the subtle but pervasive influence of naturalism can lead believers to unconsciously adopt and promote ideas that stand in direct contradiction to the Christian worldview. As we saw, when such unbiblical assumptions are left unchallenged, they don't simply remain harmless intellectual errors; they actively undermine the plausibility and credibility of the Christian worldview, especially within a culture already predisposed to skepticism. The more these naturalistic ideas go unnoticed and unaddressed, the more entrenched they become, subtly shaping the way even Christians think and speak about matters like human nature, consciousness, and now, artificial intelligence.

Because we've failed to grasp the depth of these underlying worldview issues, their influence has naturally bled into the way we approach AI. And this should give us pause. It should lead us to step back and carefully reflect on how we, as Christians, are framing conversations about AI, not just in academic settings or theological discussions but in everyday conversations and casual interactions.

As we've established throughout this chapter, consciousness is neither identical to, reducible to, nor emergent from anything physical. It is not something that arises from the mere rearrangement of matter or the complexity of physical processes. Consciousness is something fundamentally immaterial, something that belongs uniquely to immaterial souls, and, for human beings, souls made in the image of an immaterial God. Therefore, as believers, it is critical that we think biblically not only about human nature but also about AI itself. We must ensure that our view of what it means to be a person is grounded in Scripture and in a proper understanding of the soul

25. Suleyman, *Coming Wave*, 149.

26. Lennox, *2084*, 21.

and mind, not in the shifting, reductionistic assumptions of a naturalistic culture. Human beings are immaterial souls with immaterial minds, made in the image of an immaterial God. Nothing about this could ever apply to AI—not now, not in the future, not even in principle. And let's ensure that both our thinking and our language reflect that reality.

BIBLIOGRAPHY

Cooper, John W. *Body, Soul, and Life Everlasting: Biblical Anthropology and the Monism Dualism Debate.* London: Leicester, 2000.

Hernandez, Eric. *The Lazy Approach to Evangelism: A Simple Guide for Conversing with Nonbelievers.* Dallas: GC2, 2023.

Jacobs, Alan. *How to Think: A Survival Guide for a World at Odds.* New York: Crown, 2017.

Jump, Tom, and Eric Hernandez. "Tom Jump vs Eric Hernandez—Freewill, Consciousness, and the Existence of the Soul." Eric Hernandez, May 1, 2019. YouTube video, 1:45:36. https://www.youtube.com/watch?v=m7LVr5OaSAE&t=4585s.

Lennox, John C. *2084: Artificial Intelligence and the Future of Humanity.* Grand Rapids: Zondervan Reflective, 2020.

Moreland, J. P. *The Soul: How We Know It's Real and Why It Matters.* Chicago: Moody, 2014.

Moreland, J. P., and Scott B. Rae. *Body and Soul: Human Nature and the Crisis in Ethics.* Downers Grove, IL: InterVarsity, 2000.

Moreland, J. P., and William Lane Craig. *Philosophical Foundations for a Christian Worldview.* 2nd ed. Downers Grove, IL: InterVarsity, 2017.

Nagel, Thomas. *Mind and Cosmos: Why the Materialist Neo-Darwinian Conception of Nature Is Almost Certainly False.* Oxford: Oxford University Press.

Pauly, Ryan. "Reasons to Believe in God." TJump, Mar. 2, 2024. YouTube video, 2:26:41. https://www.youtube.com/watch?v=L2VaekjzgVM.

Rickabaugh, Brandon, and J. P. Moreland. *The Substance of Consciousness: A Comprehensive Defense of Contemporary Substance Dualism.* Hoboken, NJ: Wiley-Blackwell, 2024.

Searle, John. *Minds, Brains, and Science.* Cambridge, MA: Harvard University Press, 1984.

Suleyman, Mustafa. *The Coming Wave: Technology, Power, and the Twenty-First Century's Greatest Dilemma.* New York: Crown, 2023.

2

Stewarding Technology for Human Flourishing

Ryan Pauly

It was the fall of 2006, and I was sitting in a room full of students. The class was college algebra, but I'm not sure if anyone was learning any algebra. Each student sat in the stadium-seating lecture hall with a laptop open on their desk, and many of them were being used for anything but the class topic. Movies were being watched, sports scores checked, and MySpace pages updated. I know this because I was a student watching TV shows during long and boring lectures. But it's math! Who really needs it (sorry, math teachers)?

A few years later, I found myself in a similar situation, but this time it was an Old Testament Theology class. Of the thirty students in class, only three were taking notes by hand. Of those on laptops, only two were actually taking notes. The rest were distracted by everything the internet had to offer.

Fast forward one more time. Students continued to be distracted, but I was no longer a student alongside them; I was the teacher. I taught in a school that adopted a one-to-one technology policy where every student had their own laptop in class. The textbooks were digital, tests were taken online, and technology was used for most classroom activities. The idea was that this was needed to prepare students for the technological world they were about to enter. The problem: technology had become more of a distraction and a hindrance than a tool. I caught students shopping during tests, watching movies, checking social media, texting their friends, and using AI to write papers. I took away more cell phones than I could count. It became normal to have students staring at their screens and laughing while I was trying to teach. This resulted in teachers making new rules where notes had to be taken on paper, phones were turned in at the beginning of each class, and physical textbooks were brought back into the classroom.

Were we fighting the inevitable? Should we have accepted the new world in which we live and adapted to a new teaching approach? Mustafa Suleyman, a leading AI researcher and cofounder of DeepMind, an AI company acquired by Google, recognizes that for those who spend time in the tech or policy circles, "It quickly becomes obvious that head-in-the-sand is the default ideology."[1] Christians are not called to put their heads in the sand and adopt technology without thinking. Does this mean that we fight back by withdrawing from our technological culture? That doesn't seem like a better option to me. I want to encourage believers to have a positive theological vision for their technology use so they can live productive lives *in* our technological society, not apart from it.

WHAT IS TECHNOLOGY?

At the most basic level, technology can be defined as "the human activity of using tools to transform God's creation for practical purposes."[2] God has created us to be stewards of his world, and technology allows us to live out that God-given calling. This includes much more than our electronic devices. Even shovels, hammers, and other tools are considered forms of technology.

Then there's artificial intelligence. This is "an emerging field of technology defined as non-biological intelligence, where a machine is programmed to accomplish complex goals by applying knowledge to the task at hand."[3] This type of technology surrounds us every day as it functions in our smartphones, social media, smart-home devices, and more. "Take Netflix and Amazon, for example. Both companies use highly advanced

1. Suleyman, *Coming Wave*, 31.
2. Dyer, *From the Garden*, 82–83.
3. Thacker, *Age of AI*, 23–24.

algorithms and AI systems to recommend movies and products to keep us engaged with their platforms."[4] Suleyman describes it as the "new electricity." He says, "Like electricity it will be an on-demand utility that permeates and powers almost every aspect of daily life, society, the economy: a general-purpose technology embedded everywhere."[5] In this sense, Suleyman argues, "AI isn't really 'emerging' anymore. It's in products, services, and devices you use every day."[6]

IS TECHNOLOGY NEUTRAL?

One of the biggest misconceptions about technology is that it is neutral. When I ask students if technology is neutral, the overwhelming response is "yes!" Since it can be used for good or for evil, technology itself is neutral. All that matters is how we use it, right? Not exactly. Technology is never neutral because "regardless of whether we use them for good or evil, the act of using them forms us physically, mentally, spiritually, and relationally."[7] In fact, John Dyer, who serves as the VP for enrollment and educational technology and professor of theological studies at Dallas Theological Seminary, thinks that believing technology is neutral is one of the most dangerous things you can believe in this world.[8] The reason is that this belief often shields us from the true effects of technology.

If you grew up in a Christian home like me, then you probably had restrictions when it came to technology and entertainment. Parents often, and for good reason, shield their children from online content containing cursing, violence, nudity, and witchcraft. This is good, but it's only one way that we are influenced by technology. It is only taking into account morality. Samuel James, author of *Digital Liturgies*, writes that we can "faithfully avoid vulgar and explicit content on the web while simultaneously being shaped by it in a profoundly sub-Christian way."[9] The moral use of technology is only one key factor. There are also questions on how technology is shaping reality and changing us.

4. Thacker, *Age of AI*, 29.
5. Suleyman, *Coming Wave*, 145.
6. Suleyman, *Coming Wave*, 83.
7. Dyer, *From the Garden*, 21.
8. Dyer, *From the Garden*, 18.
9. James, *Digital Liturgies*, 17.

Take a shovel for example. Dyer mentions that there are both good and bad uses of a shovel. You can use a shovel to dig holes and create a beautiful garden, or you can also use a shovel to bury stolen goods. However, the fact that you are digging holes in the ground means that you are changing reality as you move dirt, and the digging affects you by strengthening your muscles or even causing blisters.[10] All technology affects us and our world, but unlike shovels, the power of AI means that digital technologies have a far greater effect.

There are a few big differences between digital technologies and household technologies like tools. Let's compare a phone and a shovel. First, shovels are disconnected, whereas phones are constantly connected. Companies make money when you buy a shovel, but they don't continue to profit from our use of them as they do with phones. "In other words, there is no one inside our shovels trying to get us to dig more holes, but there are people on the other side of our phones who profit each time we pick them up!"[11] Phones are always crying "Pick me up!" through notifications, while shovels sit there and wait for you to use them.

Second, digital technologies are often more addictive. Tristan Harris is a technology ethicist and cofounded the Center for Humane Technology. He commented in an article, "When you open up the blue Facebook icon, you're activating the AI, which tries to figure out the perfect thing it can show you that'll engage you. It doesn't have any intelligence, except figuring out what gets the most clicks."[12] The more you engage, the more money they make. This means that application creators have an incentive to get you to be on your device as much as possible.

Third, newer digital technologies are often omni-use. This means that they can be used for multiple purposes. Subsequently, it is almost impossible to know if someone is working, searching for answers, texting friends, playing games, or a wide range of other possibilities when using a phone. The same is not true of a shovel.

You may be excited about all of the possibilities now available with developments in AI, but we must proceed with caution. Technology is not neutral, and it alters the way that we live. Dyer believes that "AI may be the source of the most challenging theological and ethical questions of this

10. Dyer, *From the Garden*, 190.

11. Dyer, *From the Garden*, 77.

12. Klein, "How Technology Is Designed," para. 9.

century."[13] Suleyman has been on the front lines of researching AI and comments that "as the technology has progressed over the years, my concerns have grown."[14] In his book *The Coming Wave: Technology, Power, and the Twenty-first Century's Greatest Dilemma*, he comments that each new advancement in technology comes in like a wave. The difference now is that this wave of AI is more like a tsunami, and it could destroy us if we are not ready.

THE POSITIVE AND NEGATIVE OF AI

There are many positives to AI. John Lennox writes that his commitment to the biblical worldview allows him to be thankful to God for the developments in AI. AI has brought hope to people in a damaged world by "giving hearing to the deaf, sight to the blind, limbs to the limbless; eradicating killer diseases; and benefiting from a host of other things that represent magnificent work in the spirit of a Creator who has made humans in his image to be creative themselves."[15]

AI advances in the medical arena are mind-blowing and beneficial to patients. Researchers have been able to create prosthetic limbs that are controlled by thought.[16] We have seen AI systems that aid doctors in their diagnoses and procedures. Unlike doctors who have jobs that demand their attention, AI can "scour massive amounts of patient data from across the world to provide doctors with better insights with which to care for patients."[17] This includes the latest research and published journal articles that doctors don't have time to read. AI is helping develop new drugs. Another AI system was able to look at thousands of healthy and diseased eyes to more accurately diagnose eye conditions.[18] Smartwatches can recognize seizures, and some digital assistants are "trained" in speech recognition "to give early warning of possible self-harming or even suicidal tendencies in their users."[19]

13. Dyer, *From the Garden*, 206.
14. Suleyman, *Coming Wave*, 23.
15. Lennox, *2084*, 145.
16. Thacker, *Age of AI*, 55.
17. Thacker, *Age of AI*, 64.
18. Lennox, *2084*, 56.
19. Lennox, *2084*, 55.

Most of us use AI every day, like Siri and Alexa, to give quick answers to questions we don't care to remember. Digital assistance tools allow us to complete work quickly or even communicate with people over a language barrier. Suleyman believes that these technologies "will make life easier, healthier, more productive, and more enjoyable for billions. They will save time, cost, hassle, and millions of lives. The significance of this should not be trivialized or forgotten amid the uncertainty."[20]

While it's important to recognize the positive impact of AI, we must also come to terms with its negative effects. AI systems have led to job loss and issues in job recruitment. Knowing that people are longing for human interaction, 1st Bank in Colorado put out a commercial for their new technology called "Sara," which is a real person who can help with your banking needs. We laugh at their joke but realize what they're getting at when AI is managing 85 percent of customer inquiries.[21] It is yet another reminder of how far AI has come. Depersonalization is just one negative. The negative effects of AI could be extreme if these powerful tools are used for malicious purposes. The AI system that can search for cures to rare diseases can be flipped and optimized to look for killers instead.

THE SHAPING POWER OF TECHNOLOGY

We have seen what we are doing with it, but what is it doing to us? What I hope to communicate is that while there are positive and negative uses of technology, our theology of technology must explore the ways that technology transforms individuals and communities. Dyer lists four things that technology does.[22]

First, technology can extend or magnify something we do naturally. Think of a microphone that allows you to communicate in ways that you wouldn't be able to do naturally, or telescopes that let you see what the naked eye could not.

Second, technology can eliminate or amputate something that we used to do. Think of advances in heating and air conditioning. I lived in the Dominican Republic for four years, where it was very hot and my house didn't have air conditioning. What was the result? I spent time outside and got to know my neighbors. AC has eliminated our need to cool down outside

20. Suleyman, *Coming Wave*, 180.

21. Lennox, *2084*, loc. 64.

22. Dyer, *From the Garden*, 119.

and, for many, has turned neighbors into strangers. "The device had hidden the process of cooling that used to take place outside, and the result was that the space where people used to commune became obsolete."[23] Central heating is another example. Before the heater, a family would have to gather around the living room fireplace to stay warm. "Technology literally decentralized homelife, laying the technical foundation for the everyone-has-their-own-bedroom layout of a home that we assume today."[24] To be clear, central heating and air conditioning aren't evil. Those who have it know how much of an incredible blessing it is on a hot summer day or a cold winter night, and we should thank God for giving people the knowledge and ability to create such technologies, but it's imperative to recognize what these technologies are doing to us.

Third, technology can retrieve something from the past. There was a time when you were able to connect with everyone you knew because they lived close by. Transportation technologies and the growing job market have caused people to move away for work, which has resulted in fractured relationships and dislocated communication. Our communication technologies allow us to connect once again like we are living close together. My immediate family is spread out over four different states, but we can FaceTime and connect in ways that were unavailable in the past. At the same time, these technologies often hinder us from connecting with those who live close by. This has radically changed our understanding of community. No longer is your community the people that live around you.

Fourth, technology can reverse into a more negative behavior when it's overused. I was giving a lecture to a group of students in California, where I went over the effects of amusement culture. I commented on how the overindulgence of amusement technologies can enslave our affections. It can turn our companionship into defiance, respect into disrespect, helpfulness into aggression, and other-centeredness into self-centeredness.[25] As the night came to an end, one student approached me to say that he uses this framework to judge his video game usage. When he starts being frustrated and aggressive towards his mother when she asks for help, then he knows it's time for a break.

This is not simply a content issue for believers. Samuel James, the author of *Digital Liturgies*, writes that "evangelicals have often focused

23. Dyer, *From the Garden*, 233.

24. James, *Digital Liturgies*, 44.

25. Myers, *Understanding the Culture*, 177–82.

exclusively on the content that our TVs, computers, and smartphones deliver to us rather than the form by which that content is delivered."[26] I agree that we need to have boundaries for certain content that our children can and can't consume, but we shouldn't stop there. The mere existence of these digital technologies has recalibrated our worldviews and reshaped our consciences.[27]

WHAT DOES IT MEAN TO FLOURISH?

The Worldview of Technology

Now that we have a better understanding of what technology is and what it's doing to us, we can then turn our attention to human flourishing. "One of the reasons so few people can articulate the effects of the online world is that so few people have a baseline standard of human flourishing."[28] Have you heard the common phrase, "We know we are sick because we know what it means to be healthy"? The pain I am currently experiencing in my knee is a problem because I know that pain tells me something is wrong. But when it comes to technology, how do we know if we are using it well if we don't know what it looks like to live well?

Many technologies are created to make life easier, more convenient, healthier, more productive, or more enjoyable. These are not bad things, but if we are not careful, we can allow technology to recalibrate our worldview to where ease, convenience, and productivity become our highest values. We answer the question, "What is the good life?" based on the values and purposes of technology instead of Scripture. Is the highest goal a life of ease, or is there value to working hard and struggling through a task? Romans 5:3–4 tells us that we can "rejoice in our sufferings, knowing that suffering produces endurance, and endurance produces character, and character produces hope."[29] If a life of ease is the highest value or end goal, then why would we rejoice in our sufferings? Suffering and perseverance are the opposite of ease.

26. James, *Digital Liturgies*, 41–42.

27. James, *Digital Liturgies*, 37.

28. James, *Digital Liturgies*, 23.

29. Unless otherwise noted, all Scripture in this chapter is quoted from the English Standard Version (ESV).

What about convenience? As a family of four with two sons under three years old, we are grateful for our many modern conveniences. It is a blessing to have Amazon ship anything we need to the house or to get a quick drive-up order of groceries on our way home. But while these services can be a blessing for many and even necessary for some, we should still reflect on the ways that they are shaping us. "What are we sacrificing in the name of convenience and saving time? What if household chores or family errands are actually meaningful?"[30] A trip to the grocery store can be tough with small children, but it can also be valuable. I try to take the opportunity to quiz my children about their fruits and vegetables as we walk around the store. My older son likes to play basketball by throwing the oranges or apples into the little bags. They can also learn the importance of waiting in line, earning money to purchase needs, and having face-to-face conversations with those working in the store. Going back and understanding how things are made or where things come from can be a meaningful practice that we miss when everything shows up at our door already done.

Modern technology is all about immediacy. From "One Click" purchases on Amazon to streaming on demand, technology presents human flourishing as getting what we want as quickly as possible. If our highest value is immediacy, then values such as patience or delayed gratification would go against our understanding of what it means to flourish. Is it possible that "human innovation satisfies human comforts but starves human hearts"?[31] James put it this way: "Our digital technology has imported its values of immediacy and fleetingness into our souls. This results in more amazing products and greater feelings of efficiency and control over our world but at the high cost of a suffocating sense of anxiety."[32] Our use of technology is having a greater impact on us than we may want to admit.

Many other values of technology shape our understanding of human flourishing, but let's finish by looking at efficiency. Advances in technology make us more efficient and give us the feeling of flourishing as we optimize every moment for efficiency, particularly, the efficiency of time. My family took a trip to Colorado while I was researching for this chapter. We decided to go to the lake one morning, and while my older son played in the sand, my younger son took his nap on me. My first thought once he fell asleep was "I wish I had my Kindle so I could read. Oh, wait! I have the Kindle

30. Thacker, *Age of AI*, 83.

31. Reinke, *God, Technology, and Christian Life*, 178.

32. James, *Digital Liturgies*, 159.

app on my phone!" But then I instantly thought, "Why do I feel the need to fill these thirty minutes with more research instead of resting and soaking in the beauty of God's creation?" The irony is that the book I was reading was *The Shallows: What the Internet Is Doing to Our Brains* by Nicholas Carr. He argues that the internet shapes our brains with the desire to fill every moment, where we have the "inability to pay attention to one thing for more than a couple of minutes."[33] He said, "But my brain, I realized, wasn't just drifting. It was hungry. It was demanding to be fed in the way the Net fed it—and the more it was fed, the hungrier it became."[34] Does this sound more like flourishing or an addiction that needs to be satisfied? Do we yearn to be connected at every spare moment from the line at the store, waiting for food at dinner, or even at every red light? I know I constantly have to fight the urge to maximize my time by being on my device while other things are happening around me.

A Biblical Worldview

Christians recognize that we need wisdom when it comes to our technology use, and this means living in a way that lines up with reality. James writes,

> If we want to live wisely according to Scripture, then we have to live in alignment with reality. Yet, throughout Scripture and throughout human history, fallen, sinful people have used technology to try to invent an alternative reality for themselves, a reality meant to "liberate" them from the fear of the Lord and conformity to his revealed character.[35]

Without the knowledge of God and the wisdom to live in a way that aligns with God's created world, it is difficult to understand whether technology is helping or hurting human flourishing.

Our understanding of human flourishing should be formed by knowledge from God's world (general revelation) and God's word (special revelation). General revelation is available to everyone. We all can look at the effects of technology on mental health or human value and know that something needs to change. "All of these corrections operate at the level of general revelation. You don't need to know the wisdom of God or the

33. Carr, *Shallows*, loc. 16.
34. Carr, *Shallows*, 16.
35. James, *Digital Liturgies*, 31.

meaning of life to make these adjustments."[36] But again, as Christians, we shouldn't stop here. We also have the benefit of wisdom that comes from Scripture. This includes placing technology within the biblical metanarrative of creation, fall, and redemption, allowing our natures as created beings to impact our use of technology. This is why we now turn to Scripture.

CREATION

God Created

The biblical story starts by labeling God as the Creator, and this is hugely significant when we think about our natures as humans. Genesis 1:27 says,

> So God created man in his own image,
> in the image of God he created him;
> male and female he created them.

Notice the repetition of "create" three times in one verse. We clearly see God as the Creator and us as created. "Our identity, who we truly are is God-given, not man-made. God grants people the honor of living out and cultivating their identity, but not a license to ultimately design and to create it."[37] Since God is the Creator of all things (Gen 1:1, John 1:3, Col 1:16–17), we must look to him to understand how he created us.

Think of any piece of technology around you. Each one is created for a reason and functions best when used according to its design. Misuse will likely destroy it. So, what do we do? Instead of asking, "What can I do with this technology?" we should ask, "What *should* I do?" This implies a right and wrong way to use something based on its design and reflects a desire to use it rightly.

The same is true with our lives. As created beings who were created for a reason, flourishing isn't about doing whatever you want but living according to our design. You were created to know God and make him known. "God wields you for his final purposes. God made you for an end that he set in place."[38] Alternate stories replace the Creator with evolution, which results in you being the ultimate authority over your life. This is why a biblical approach to technology has to place God in his appropriate place as Creator

36. Reinke, *God, Technology, and Christian Life*, 237.
37. Ferguson, *Does God Care About Gender*, 18.
38. Reinke, *God, Technology, and Christian Life*, 67.

and us as created. In other words, as James says, "Christian wisdom tells me that I am not the final authority on myself. I am not self-created or self-sustaining, and therefore, I cannot create my own meaning and purposes out of life."[39] This is where Christian wisdom begins, but it doesn't end here.

Humans Are Set Apart

The doctrine of creation not only shows us that humans are created, but we are the pinnacle of God's creation. Nothing else is said to be created in the image of God. This is something that current AI research is questioning. Suleyman asks, "What if we could distill the essence of what makes us humans so productive and capable into software, into an algorithm?"[40] Technology has been developed to perform certain tasks better than humans. These are referred to as narrow AI in that they can perform one task well. They are designed to drive a car, diagnose a disease, or make predictions based on the past, but they are limited. The question is, will we ever be able to produce what is called general AI, a system that can do all that human intelligence can do? Many doubt this is possible, for a good reason.

When we look at the world around us, we can see that there is something different about humans. Machines may be able to lift more, jump higher, or run faster, but they often can't do all of them at once. Professor Lennox puts it this way, "It is one thing to make a machine that can simulate, say, a human hand lifting an object; it is a completely different thing to make a machine that can simulate the thoughts of a human when he or she is lifting an object."[41] The reason for the unlikelihood of a general AI ever being developed is that humans have something that machines will never have: a mind. Machines will get better at simulating our thoughts but will never be able to truly think. Suleyman's question of whether we can distill the essence of humans into an algorithm assumes that we are purely physical beings.

39. James, *Digital Liturgies*, 90.
40. Suleyman, *Coming Wave*, 21.
41. Lennox, *2084*, 17.

God Rested

God, in his infinite power, finished his act of creation and rested. How much more, then, do we need to rest? Genesis 2:2–3 says, "And on the seventh day God finished his work that he had done, and he rested on the seventh day from all his work that he had done. So God blessed the seventh day and made it holy, because on it God rested from all his work that he had done in creation." We can also look at the example of Jesus. He frequently withdrew to solitary places and got away from the crowds. While God is not resting due to physical limitations, we see that God built patterns of rest into his creation.

Times of rest are not a bad thing that need to be filled with more work. Instead, we are created to rest as our Creator rested. When was the last time you rested to celebrate what you have accomplished or to remember your freedom in Christ? Or are you more like me and move instantly to the next project as soon as one is complete? "Today we have an amazing array of time-saving devices, and yet when we never rest from them, we need to ask if they are truly our liberators or if we have allowed them to keep us enslaved."[42] Dyer goes on to say that, "if we realize that spending too much time on social media invites narcissism and that reading online too much limits deep thinking, we may not be living in the freedom of Sabbath, and we may need to reinstitute some limits."[43]

We Are Relational

We are created by a relational God to be in a relationship with him and others. We read about Jesus being challenged by the Pharisees in Matt 22:34–40. They wanted to test him by asking, "Teacher, which is the great commandment of the Law?" Jesus responded, "'You shall love the Lord your God with all your heart and with all your soul and with all your mind.' This is the great and first commandment. And a second is like it: 'You shall love your neighbor as yourself.' On these two commandments depend all the Law and the Prophets." We are created to love God and love others. This is what it looks like to live a life of flourishing.

42. Dyer, *From the Garden*, 53–54.

43. Dyer, *From the Garden*, 251.

Unfortunately, technology can separate us from others and from God.[44] Think of it this way: "The New Testament repeatedly affirms the fullness and completeness that only comes from being physically together, sharing embodied, face-to-face interaction."[45] Now ask yourself, is that a value of technology? Our goal with technology should be to use it to increase the amount that we are physically together, not as a replacement for it.

God created us with physical bodies, and this is a good part of the creation story. Therefore, our embodied existence with other embodied humans is a good gift as relational beings. While talking on FaceTime and keeping up to date with people over social media can be good, it cannot be a replacement for physical presence. Unfortunately, many people see digital relationships as being just as good or even better than being with people physically. Why? It may come from the fact that many of us don't know why it matters that we are embodied. Rather than seeing physical presence as a created good, we either see it as unimportant or problematic. "In fact, it's easy to get the impression of the opposite, that many of us see our embodiment as an obstacle to be overcome, a limitation to be transcended, or even a necessary evil to be suppressed."[46] This couldn't be further from the biblical truth as our embodied existence and physical presence with others is a good aspect of being created by a relational God for relationships.

Technology Is a Good Gift

Right after God created male and female, we read, "And God blessed them. And God said to them, 'Be fruitful and multiply and fill the earth and subdue it, and have dominion over the fish of the sea and over the birds of the heavens and over every living thing that moves on the earth" (Gen 1:28). The act of ruling, having dominion, and stewarding God's creation requires human activity and the use of tools.

We see technology playing a significant role in the biblical story. Building the temple was a technology to aid in worshiping God. Another example is when God commanded Noah to build the ark. "In the ark, God took human technology and wrote it into the grand story of redemption."[47] We also see the need for technology to fulfill our calling and live out the

44. Reinke, *God, Technology, and Christian Life*, 282.

45. Dyer, *From the Garden*, 250.

46. James, *Digital Liturgies*, 34.

47. Reinke, *God, Technology, and Christian Life*, 44.

Great Commission. We see advances like airplanes, boats, and cars to be hugely beneficial in our attempt to "go therefore and make disciples of all nations, baptizing them in the name of the Father and of the Son and of the Holy Spirit" (Matt 28:19). We are called to cultivate God's good creation, and technology is implemented to accomplish this creation mandate. However, we also know that we are fallen, and our brokenness infects everything, including our technology use.

THE FALL

If the ark is an example of technology being written into the grand story of redemption, the tower of Babel is an example of technology being used to circumvent God. With the ark, God commanded the use of technology and protected Noah during the building process. "But in Babel, God squashed it. In the face of human self-glory, he introduced tensions that utterly thwarted human collaboration."[48] While Scripture never calls technology evil, we get a clear picture of our fallen nature and how it infects everything.

Broken vs. Designed Features

When people discuss the ethics of using technology to change our bodies, you often hear them asking whether the change is restorative or enhancement to determine ethical value. The fall has resulted in bodily issues like our eyes going bad or our organs, joints, or bones failing. When innovation is used to restore these broken features, we are doing something good. Glasses or contact lenses for people like myself are an incredible gift from God as I can clearly see the words I am typing on the screen.

The problem is when we start to see all of our limitations or issues as a result of the fall, as something to overcome. The fact is that God designed us with limitations. Being tired is not a flaw in our nature that needs to be overcome with technology but is a designed feature. Instead of using design features like night and day to be a pattern of rest and wake, our technology allows us to work and be productive at all hours of the day. The same technologies that are designed to make life easier and more efficient tempt us to overwork and keep us from resting. We have always been tempted to overwork, and technology allows us to do this.

48. Reinke, *God, Technology, and Christian Life*, 44.

Since we are not infinite, all-powerful beings, we are designed with weaknesses. Biblically, these weaknesses are used to show our need and dependence on God. Paul writes about a thorn in his flesh in 2 Cor 12:1–10. This thorn was given to "keep [him] from becoming conceited." When he pleaded with the Lord that it should leave, God responded, "My grace is sufficient for you, for my power is made perfect in weakness." Paul concluded, "I am content with weakness, insults, hardships, persecutions, and calamities. For when I am weak, then I am strong." Technology can give us the illusion that all weaknesses can and should be overcome and that we no longer need to depend on God.

Our Desire to Become Like God

Scripture gives the account of the fall in Gen 3. We see the serpent begin by challenging Eve, saying, "You will not surely die. For God knows that when you eat of it your eyes will be opened, and you will be like God, knowing good and evil." The serpent misrepresented God and caused Eve to question God's goodness. "This momentous event, often called the Fall, happened when human beings began to think of themselves as more than the image of God and desire to be a god: 'you will be like God.' In a word, Homo deus."[49] This line of thinking that led to the original sin, Thacker believes, is present in modern technology and AI. He believes "technology can fool us into thinking we are something that we are not. That we are in control. That we are mini gods."[50] He is not the only one who sees this as a temptation of technology.

Yuval Noah Harari is a historian from Oxford University and a *New York Times* bestselling author who wrote the book *Homo Deus*, where he argued that advances in technology have solved many of humanity's problems, like famine, plague, and war. So where do we go from here? He writes, "And having raised humanity above the beastly level of survival struggles, we will now aim to upgrade humans into gods, and turn Homo sapiens into Homo deus."[51] His idea is that we are in control and we are solving the problems of the world through technology, so why not assume that we can solve every human problem?

49. Lennox, *2084*, 140.
50. Thacker, *Age of AI*, 146.
51. Harari, *Homo Deus*, 21.

It is the fall that twists our command to rule and steward creation to *control* of creation. Rather than submitting to God's sovereignty and following him, we desire to dominate and determine our own fate. Reinke believes this is a temptation of technology that feeds into our broken nature. He writes, "Technology promises to give us more control, and more control promises to give us more happiness. But the desire to control our lives is an illusory promise. We will never be in control. We will never become gods over anything, not even over ourselves."[52] Our desire for control and the Fall's effect on our technology use have serious detrimental effects. It is to this point that we now turn.

The Fall's Effects on Technology Use

We've already seen the temptation to give human qualities to objects. In return, we often begin to treat humans as things.[53] When many of the technological advances are created for the purpose of entertainment, then we can start to see people as our entertainment. In our culture, we are often the center, and everything is created to make my life more exciting. We have become accustomed to being able to mute or delete things that make us uncomfortable. The result is treating people as mutable, which leads us to become less tolerant of friends who voice opinions we dislike.[54] Humans are not technology and should not be treated as such.

Sociological research suggests that the younger generation is one of the loneliest generations. Sherry Turkle, a sociologist and licensed clinical psychologist at MIT, has been studying the effects of technology. In her book *Alone Together*, Turkle argues that "networked, we are together, but so lessened are our expectations of each other that we feel utterly alone. And there is the risk that we come to see others as objects to be accessed—and only for the parts we find useful, comforting, or amusing."[55] Her overall premise is that "we ask less of people and more of technology."[56] The argument has always been that social media allows us to connect. That is sometimes true. I also think that James is right when he says, "As much as we might tell ourselves that we go to the internet and social media to be

52. Reinke, *God, Technology, and Christian Life*, 179.

53. Turkle, *Alone Together*.

54. James, *Digital Liturgies*, 66.

55. Turkle, *Alone Together*, 154.

56. Turkle, *Alone Together*, 231.

plugged into what's going on in the world, many times we're logging on to escape it."[57]

I have found this to be true in my own life. Why do I have such a pull to scroll through social media while spending time with my sons? There are legitimate connections that technology allows us to have, but is the "bored scroll" one of them? Mindlessly looking at photos of connections that don't matter is taking me away from quality time with the people who do matter. Not only does this affect our relationships, but it has a serious impact on mental health.

Jean M. Twenge, a professor of psychology at San Diego State University, wrote the book *iGen: Why Today's Super-Connected Kids Are Growing Up Less Rebellious, More Tolerant, Less Happy—and Completely Unprepared for Adulthood*. She shares a lot of her research on teen mental health, its correlation with technology, and the increase in suicide. She writes that

> 46% more teens killed themselves in 2015 than in 2007. The rise occurred just as new-media screen time started to increase and in-person social activities began to wane. . . . With teens spending more hours with their phones and less with their friends, more are becoming depressed and committing suicide and fewer are committing homicide.[58]

This can be due in part to the isolating effects of technology, but there is another mental health crisis as a result of social media companies.

Back in 2021, Jonathan Haidt wrote an article titled "The Dangerous Experiment on Teen Girls," where he talked about the relationship between teen mental health and social media. He cited studies showing that there has been an increase in teen suicide (both sexes), self-harm (for girls only), and a large increase in anxiety and depression. This major increase began around 2010 when about 63 percent of high school students reported using "social networking sites" daily. He quoted one 2017 British study where Instagram scored as the most harmful platform in affecting teens' anxiety, loneliness, body image, and sleep.[59]

Much more could be said, but I think the data speaks for itself. Our fallen human nature and misuse of technology have had an extremely detrimental effect on human flourishing. We are lonely, distracted, anxious, and depressed, and suicide rates are rising. This is a result of believing that

57. James, *Digital Liturgies*, 41.

58. Twenge, *iGen*, 107–8.

59. Haidt, "Dangerous Experiment on Teen Girls."

we are in control of our lives and a high value placed on expressive individualism, rather than seeing ourselves as created beings who are made to be in community. The good news of the biblical story is that God did not leave us in our brokenness but initiated a plan of redemption, a plan that even applies to our technology use.

REDEMPTION

You don't have to be a Christian to realize that our world and bodies are broken. The world isn't the way it is supposed to be, and we long for it to be fixed. But where is our hope? Do we only need greater advances in technology, or are we broken beyond self-repair and in need of something far greater? God not only sent us a Savior but he has given us a place to know him, learn who we are, and experience a community to help us live a life of flourishing. I am referring to the church.

The Church

The church is the community where we do life together, and regular attendance in this embodied community will help us resist the temptations of technology toward isolation and feelings of loneliness. Samuel James has a wonderful section on the importance of the church and the communal focus of Christian thinking. He writes,

> If "inner-ringism" is a threat on one side of the internet age, the threat on the far side might be called "lone-rangerism." The web's disembodied character powerfully distorts our perception of reality. Isolated in the presence of the screen, we become more and more turned in on ourselves. In a way, this effect of the web is what inflames all others. Left to ourselves, we don't sense when our anger and anxiety are clouding our wisdom. Left to ourselves, we can't see our slide into unthinking partisanship. The Bible is not naive about our struggle to think wisely and Christianly. God knows we are like grass. Precisely because of that, Scripture directs Christians to the heart-shaping habitat of the local church, where, through the power of the liturgy and the presence of Christ's Spirit in his people, we are formed more closely in the image of Jesus.[60]

60. James, *Digital Liturgies*, 109.

It is in the church where we learn and practice spiritual disciplines. These are practices such as prayer, fasting, solitude, silence, Bible study, and worship. These are not spiritual checklist items but are habits that grow us spiritually by pushing against our sinful desires and the temptations of technology. As Dyer puts it,

> Spiritual depth requires the ability to pray for more than a few minutes, to memorize and meditate on Scripture (not search for it online), and to love God with our hearts and our minds. This means that we must be careful to cultivate and retain the skill of deeply reading and sincerely contemplating the things of God, something that attention-getting technologies do not value. Faithfulness also requires that we can sit with a person and deeply listen without being distracted by a phone or wearable. There may be no greater Christian witness in our time than someone who can truly master the art of listening well in an age of constant interruptions.

God is using the church to restore our brokenness in this technological world. We are not created to exist in a screen-mediated world. We are called to belong, and "our pursuit of truth must take us nearer to other people and physical life, not away from it."[61]

Technology's Failed Attempt at Salvation

A technological worldview makes us believe that everything is physical, our problems are technical, and everything can be solved with better technology. We see this faulty view when Harari writes, "They don't think of death as a metaphysical mystery, and they certainly don't view death as the source of life's meaning. Rather, for modern people death is a technical problem that we can and should solve."[62] This type of thinking led him to the conclusion that "we don't need to wait for the Second Coming in order to overcome death. A couple of geeks in the lab can do it."[63] Do you see the worldview-shaping power that leads us to believe that we can become like God and be our own savior?

The problem is that technology never deals with our root failure. Our problem is not a technical problem but an alienation from God: a sin problem. Romans 5:12 says, "So death spread to all men because all sinned."

61. James, *Digital Liturgies*, 110.

62. Harari, *Homo Deus*, 22.

63. Harari, *Homo Deus*, 23.

Lennox writes, "Human death is much more than a technical problem. It is inevitable as a result of the initial rebellion of humans against God (the Fall) and the consequent removal by God of the tree of life."[64] This is why the conversation on death being the result of sin instead of a technical problem is so important. The solution can be found only after we have correctly diagnosed the problem.

God Has Overcome Death

Scripture is clear that God is sovereign over all, even determining when everyone is born and dies.[65] But life doesn't end at death. "'Remember Jesus Christ, risen from the dead . . . .' This is the key to real hope. Death is not the end."[66] Our hope is not found in technology but in the one who overcame death.

This is the beauty we read about in 1 Cor 15:52–57 when it says, "The dead will be raised imperishable, and we shall be changed. . . . Death is swallowed up in victory. O death, where is your victory? O death, where is your sting? The sting of death is sin, and the power of sin is the law. But thanks be to God, who gives us victory through our Lord Jesus Christ." It is only through the resurrection of Jesus that God will bring life to our mortal bodies (Rom 8:11). However, this isn't merely a future reality. Theologian N. T. Wright argues that salvation applies to the here and now as well. He writes, "The work of salvation, in its full sense, is (1) about whole human beings, not merely souls; (2) about the present, not simply the future; and (3) about what God does through us, not merely what God does in and for us."[67] Our views, actions, and desires should be changed now because of what Christ did in his death and resurrection.

This is the Christian hope, and it does not disappoint. "But for all of our aspirations for the future, we must see that our laudable efforts to overcome sickness and disease can have dangerous consequences if we act as if we are God or seek to upgrade ourselves into gods, turning Homo sapiens into Homo deus, a god-man. There already is a god-man, and his name is

64. Lennox, *2084*, 159.

65. "The Lord kills and brings to life; he brings down to Sheol and raises up" (1 Sam 2:6); "See now that I, even I, am he, and there is no god beside me; I kill and I make alive; I wound and I heal; and there is none that can deliver out of my hand" (Deut 32:39).

66. Lennox, *2084*, 222.

67. Wright, *Surprised by Hope*, 200.

Jesus."[68] It is for this reason that we turn our attention to the practical steps that will allow us to steward technology for human flourishing rather than to its detriment.

CHRISTIAN WISDOM IN THE PRACTICAL

What I hope you have seen in this theology of technology is that "if God is the center of your life, technology is a great gift. If technology is your savior, you're lost."[69] This is why our personal technology use must include Christian wisdom as we place technology into God's story.

Ask Questions

Asking questions means that our minds are turned on while we use new technologies. This allows us to continue thinking about its effects rather than being passive users. Here's a list of questions to consider either before or after adopting new technologies.

- Am I using this for good or evil?
- What does this do *for* me?
- What does this do *to* me?
- What does this seem to suggest humans are for?
- How does this shape reality?
- How could it affect our view of God?
- Who is paying for it?
- What do they want me to do?
- What have I gained?
- What have I lost?

68. Thacker, *Age of AI*, 60.

69. Reinke, *God, Technology, and Christian Life*, 24.

Understand the Medium

Christians are often so focused on the content of what students are consuming that we don't think of the effects of the technology itself or the medium through which we consume it. The medium can change the meaning and value of the content, as well as shape how we engage with it.

First, "older mediums tend to communicate a deeper sense of meaning and value than newer mediums do."[70] Think of a message to a friend. A text saying, "Thank you!" for a recent gift they gave you is meaningful, but many see a handwritten note as carrying more meaning. Not all mediums are the same.

Second, different mediums change how we engage. Think of music. In the past, music was a community event that brought people together. Not only did you need a band made up of different individuals, but you also had an audience there to listen. Now, listening to music is often isolating, as AirPods are designed for individual use and give off the message "Don't interrupt me" instead of "Come listen to this with me."

Reading books doesn't allow us to do much else, and we can engage deeply in the story. Reading on our phones leads to constant distractions, and notifications take our attention away from the story. The point here is our need to think deeply about the medium, not just the message.

Personal Containment

Delay adoption. While Suleyman thinks this new wave of AI can't be contained as a whole, there are absolutely things we can do for personal containment. While I don't believe we should reject technology completely, I do believe it should be delayed. Technology is clearly shaping us, and it has a stronger influence on younger kids. I talked to one parent who struggles to get his daughter to play outside because she'd rather be on her iPad. Abigail Shrier, the author of *Irreversible Damage: The Transgender Craze Seducing Our Daughters*, condenses her research into one powerful sentence when she writes,

> If I had told you in 2007 that one device would produce a sudden skyrocketing in self-harm among teens and tweens, you would likely have said, "No way is my kid getting one." And yet, here we are: the statistical explosion of bullying, cutting, anorexia,

70. Dyer, *From the Garden*, 153.

> depression, and the rise of sudden transgender identification is owed to the self-harm instructing, manipulation, abuse, and relentless harassment supplied by a single smartphone.[71]

What's her advice for our girls? Don't get your kid a smartphone.

Delaying the adoption of technology allows our students to develop biblical values first and use technology out of their convictions and values. In contrast, early adoption can enable technology to shape our values and uses. But what do we do when all of our kid's friends have the technology and our kid doesn't? Won't they be left out? This is a legitimate concern since so much socialization happens on technology, but I agree with Thacker when he writes, "But delaying the adoption of technology is not going to harm your children. It might benefit them. While they might miss out on things here and there, the value of restraint and maturity will serve your kids much more than the allure of immediacy as they grow older."[72]

Find solitude. Our young people are growing up in a world that is constantly connected. For many, there is not a moment in the day when they are disconnected. They are either always on technology, or it is always on them.[73] When is the last time you have taken a break from technology? When have you practiced the spiritual discipline of solitude and silence? Or, are you like me at the lake, wanting to fill every moment with something to feel productive? "Yes, no matter how difficult," as Turkle writes, "It is time to look again toward the virtues of solitude, deliberateness, and living fully in the moment."[74] This means being present and engaging in the world around you.

Be present. I was at the park with my son and taking pictures as he was going down the slides. While this is good to save these memories, I thought to myself, "When my son looks at me during his big life moments, will he see my eyes and a face that is proud of him or the back of my phone?" Turkle's book hit me like a ton of bricks when she wrote,

> From the youngest ages, these teenagers have associated technology with shared attention. Phones, before they become an essential element in a child's own life, were the competition, one that children didn't necessarily feel they could beat. . . . Children have always competed for their parents' attention, but this generation

71. Shrier, *Irreversible Damage*, 212.
72. Thacker, *The Age of AI*, 80–81.
73. Turkle, *Alone Together*, 17.
74. Turkle, *Alone Together*, 296.

> has experienced something new. Previously, children had to deal with parents being off with work, friends, or each other. Today, children contend with parents who are physically close, tantalizingly so, but mentally elsewhere.[75]

Most parents love their children more than their devices, yet we keep saying "wait" to our children while we scroll through what we would admit is not as important.

Take breaks. My work requires that I be online as I post content on Instagram and YouTube and interact with viewers. Because of this, I recently used the screen time feature on the iPhone to block all social media apps on Saturday and Sunday. I was shocked at how refreshing this turned out to be as I took time away from comment sections and was present with my family. Jean Twenge cites studies showing that "the kids who had spent five days away from screens improved their social skills significantly more than the control group did."[76] We are not created for constant connection, nor can we bear the weight of the world's problems. If Jesus took breaks from much more important things like healing people, how much more do we need breaks from social media feeds?

What does this look like practically? Have screen-free days during the week. Make meals a screen-free time during the day. Try to eat meals as a family when possible. Make screen-free zones in the house, like bedrooms. This will encourage students to come out of their rooms and spend time as a family. Finally, turn off your notifications for most apps. This allows you to control when you pick up your phone rather than your phone constantly calling out to you.

Technology Is for the Table

We are created for relationships, so how can we use technology to build relationships rather than isolate ourselves? John Dyer writes that everything we do with our technology "should be directed toward enriching the few, precious face-to-face encounters we have in our busy world."[77] So rather than seeing pictures of a friend's recent vacation on Instagram and moving on, maybe you could use that to call them and say something like, "I saw

75. Turkle, *Alone Together*, 267.

76. Twenge, *iGen*, 110.

77. Dyer, *From the Garden to the City*, 246.

your pictures from your vacation. That looked amazing! I'd love to get some coffee or dinner and hear all about it." Rather than using technology to view our friend's lives from a distance, think of ways to use it to be together.

CONCLUSION

God has uniquely placed us in this moment of history where we are faced with the challenges of technology. We have a moral command to love God and love our neighbors as ourselves. This means we must think long and hard about whether we are being intentional with our technology use, making sure it fits with God's design for the world rather than a false narrative. It is only when we understand how God created us and the world to function that we can use technology in a God-glorifying way that leads to our flourishing. I hope that this chapter, and the book as a whole, will give you the biblical wisdom to steward AI faithfully.

BIBLIOGRAPHY

Carr, Nicholas. *The Shallows: What the Internet Is Doing to Our Brains.* New York: W. W. Norton, 2010.

Chow, Andrew R. "ChatGPT May Be Eroding Critical Thinking Skills, According to a New MIT Study." *Time,* June 23, 2025. https://time.com/7295195/ai-chatgpt-google-learning-school/.

Dyer, John. *From the Garden to the City: The Place of Technology in the Story of God.* Grand Rapids: Kregel, 2011.

Ferguson, Samuel D. *Does God Care About Gender Identity?* Wheaton, IL: Crossway, 2023.

Haidt, Jonathan. "The Dangerous Experiment on Teen Girls." *Atlantic,* Nov. 21, 2021. https://www.theatlantic.com/ideas/archive/2021/11/facebooksdangerous-experiment-teen-girls/620767/.

Harari, Yuval Noah. *Homo Deus: A Brief History of Tomorrow.* London: Penguin Random House, 2015.

James, Samuel D. *Digital Liturgies: Rediscovering Christian Wisdom in an Online Age.* Wheaton, IL: Crossway, 2023.

Klein, Ezra. "How Technology Is Designed to Bring Out the Worst in Us." Vox, Feb. 19, 2018. https://www.vox.com/technology/2018/2/19/17020310/ tristan-harris-facebook-twitter-humane-tech-time.

Lennox, John C. *2084: Artificial Intelligence and the Future of Humanity.* Grand Rapids, MI: Zondervan Reflective, 2020.

Myers, Jeff. *Understanding the Culture: A Survey of Social Engagement.* Manitou Springs, CO: Summit Ministries, 2017.

Reinke, Tony. *God, Technology, and the Christian Life.* Wheaton, IL: Crossway, 2022.

Shrier, Abigail. *Irreversible Damage: The Transgender Craze Seducing Our Daughters.* New York: Regnery, 2020.

Suleyman, Mustafa. *The Coming Wave: Technology, Power, and the Twenty-First Century's Greatest Dilemma*. New York: Crown, 2023.

Thacker, Jason. *The Age of AI*. Grand Rapids: Zondervan, 2020.

Turkle, Sherry. *Alone Together: Why We Expect More from Technology and Less from Each Other*. New York: Basic, 2011.

Twenge, Jean M. *iGen: Why Today's Super-Connected Kids Are Growing Up Less Rebellious, More Tolerant, Less Happy—and Completely Unprepared for Adulthood*. New York: Atria, 2017.

Wright, N. T. *Surprised by Hope: Rethinking Heaven, the Resurrection, and the Mission of the Church*. New York: HarperCollins, 2008.

3

Stewarding ChatGPT

A Dangerous New Form of Plagiarism

Brian G. Chilton, PhD

In the classic 2008 Disney film *WALL-E*, humanity is given a glimpse at what could be their future.[1] The movie depicts a futuristic, seemingly utopian society in which technology meets every whim and fancy of human beings. Due to abhorrent conditions on Earth, human society lives in spaceships hovering over the world and seated in technologically guided chairs. Though the culture appeared to be a utopian society at first glance, the movie later revealed that the technological advances of AI governed humanity with a dystopian rule. Rather than being served by their technological devices, humans were ruled by their technological devices. People of this futuristic age had lost most of their muscle mass, to the point that they were no longer able to walk by their own power. Furthermore, they could no longer think for themselves. A little rogue robot named WALL-E reminded humanity of their need to become self-sufficient and to care for the needs of their planet.

While this animated film may seem to be a bit far-fetched, it is not as improbable as one might imagine. In the prophetic book *Amusing Ourselves to Death*, Neal Postman warns that an overreliance on technology can

1. Stanton, *WALL-E*.

detract from times of reflection and critical thinking. Postman encourages people to converse with the ideas of their culture and time. He says,

> I use the word 'conversation' metaphorically to refer not only to speech but to all techniques and technologies that permit people of a particular culture to exchange messages. In this sense, all culture is a conversation or, more precisely, a corporation of conversations, conducted in a variety of symbolic modes.[2]

Postman warns that technological advances, while beneficial, come with an inherent series of responsibilities and cautions that

> such interpositions of media is that their role in directing what we will see or know is so rarely noticed. A person who reads a book or who watches television or glances at his watch is not usually interested in how his mind is organized and controlled by these events, still less in what idea of the world is suggested by a book, television, or a watch.[3]

Postman was not against technology, rather, he was against the over-indulgence in media to the point that a person is no longer able to organize their thoughts and reflect on what they read or believe.

You might be thinking that Postman wrote his piece in the twenty-first century amid all the harbingers associated with AI.[4] If that's what you think, then you would be wrong. Postman wrote in the mid-80s during the time of the Reagan administration. AI was not at the forefront of everyone's mind at the time. However, Postman, in an almost prophetic tone, observed and acknowledged the direction that human critical thinking was headed. And he was spot on with his assessment.

Fast-forward forty years, and Postman's concerns are even more troubling. Today, we bear witness to the advance of a technology known as ChatGPT. ChatGPT is a writing tool directed by AI. ChatGPT is actually only one of a large body of generative writing apps. Other generative writing apps include Jasper AI, ChatGPT, Claude, Copilot, SEO.ai, Sudowrite, Rytr.me, Chibi AI, Frase, Anyword, INK for All, and Copysmith, to name a few.[5] Before moving on, it must be noted that this chapter will use two

2. Postman, *Amusing Ourselves to Death*, 6.

3. Postman, *Amusing Ourselves to Death*, 11.

4. AI speaks of artificial intelligence.

5. For more information on these alternate writing apps and to see additional generative writings apps not on this list, see Michaels, "15 AI Writing and Content."

acronyms to address forms of knowledge: AI stands for artificial intelligence, whereas NI represents human natural intelligence.[6] ChatGPT[7] can be used to write emails, memos, and chapters. One of the most problematic aspects of technology is that students can use ChatGPT to write chapters for class assignments by simply adding a prompt.[8]

Herein lies the problem. When ChatGPT, or any technology for that matter, is used to cheat, falsify, and mislead others into thinking that AI-developed documents arose from NI, then the use of the technology is morally unethical. Thus, this chapter advances the argument that the irresponsible use of ChatGPT and other forms of artificial intelligence (AI) to write documents while claiming them as original to the writer's natural intelligence (NI) is a modern form of plagiarism and creates a dangerous precedent for future generations of writers and students.

As a caveat, let it be known that I am not dismissing the importance of technological advancement. I am appreciative of modern technology, especially within the medical field. As one who suffers from sleep apnea, I know that my life has been extended with the use of my CPAP machine. It may also surprise you that I think that ChatGPT and AI can both have a positive role in research. Nonetheless, this chapter is focused more on the ethical use of these technologies, regardless of what that technology might be.

Even when writing this book, some feared that our material will be outdated as soon as the book is published due to the speed at which AI technology is progressing. In a way, such sentiments are true. So, for that reason, the chapter (as well as our book) focuses more on the practical and ethical dilemmas that arise from the overdependence on generative writing apps. The chapter will argue against any form of plagiarism due to the importance of the virtues of truth and honesty[9] and will show why the abuses of ChatGPT or any generative writing app should be considered plagiarism. Furthermore, the chapter notes the dangers associated with an

6. Sometimes, natural intelligence is sometimes abbreviated as HUMINT for human intelligence.

7. As previously noted, there are many generative writing apps on the market. This chapter will use ChatGPT as an archetype to speak of all generative writing apps used for ghostwriting documents.

8. I think you can see where this is heading. ChatGPT has the potential to be used for malevolent uses by students who want an easy passing grade.

9. This portion of the chapter will rely heavily on the virtue ethics of St. Thomas Aquinas.

overreliance on ChatGPT,[10] before concluding with some proposed ethical uses of the technology. Let's begin by defining what we mean by ChatGPT and plagiarism in general.

DEFINITIONS: WHAT IS MEANT BY PLAGIARISM AND CHATGPT?

In a humorous twist of events, my wife and I were driving to the beach for our annual vacation. For long trips, she insists that she drives, because, in her words, "I want to get to our destination within a reasonable time." According to her, my driving is mainly good for Sunday afternoons as I often drive much slower than she would desire. There are benefits to this situation as I often find myself catching up on some reading while riding in the passenger seat, with the occasional responsibilities of a navigator.

On one particular trip, the GPS gave some contradictory information, so I pulled up the GPS on my phone for further help. The GPS on the car called for a right turn, whereas the GPS on my phone called for a left turn. After giving her directions suggested by the phone, I resumed reading my book. My wife inquired, "The phone did direct us to take a left turn, right?" "Right," I responded. She looked at me and said, "Left?" I nodded and said, "Right." After reaching the intersection, I noticed that she had taken a right turn. I asked, "Why did you take a right turn? We were supposed to have taken a left." Frustrated, she retorted, "You said, 'right.'" Scratching my head, I explained, "No, I only said 'right' to agree with you when you asked if we were to take a left turn." Needless to say, I was not the favored person in the car for a while.

To assess a truth claim of any sort, Peter Kreeft reminds us that one must first "define our terms so that we understand what we mean, and . . . [demand] that we give good reasons, arguments, proofs."[11] Keeping in step with the demands of logic, it would behoove us to list out what is meant by ChatGPT in further detail as well as plagiarism.

10. And AI as a whole.

11. Kreeft, *Socratic Logic*, 7.

ChatGPT: A Trick or Treat?

ChatGPT is a chatbot program that uses AI to generate open dialogue.[12] OpenAI initially created the program.[13] ChatGPT is able to answer questions in real-time, solve mathematical equations, offer a translation from one language to another, debug and fix codes, write stories and poems, and organize and outline data.[14] With the program, people have been able to create new logos, 3D animations, compose songs, learn how to make music, and write an entire book in one day.[15]

The speed by which the application can create original pieces of literature, music, and art is nothing short of amazing. The speed at which AI calculates data will only increase, especially with the advent of quantum computing.[16] Mark my words, quantum computing will only further advance the brilliance of AI technology. Physicist Michio Kaku already calls today's computers "classical," as they use transistors and bytes and are already out-of-date when compared to quantum computers and their use of qubits.[17] Thus, when this chapter speaks of ChatGPT, it addresses any generative writing program of any ilk or type—both those that are currently used and those that will come through advanced technology.

To borrow the vernacular of Halloween, is ChatGPT a trick or a treat? The answer depends on who you ask. For some, ChatGPT is an invaluable asset for academia and the way forward for the future. Some have claimed that ChatGPT should be incorporated into a student's work.[18]

Not everyone has been as receptive of generative AI. One example is Professor Steven Mintz, professor at the University of Texas at Austin, who claimed that AI could be removing our humanity.[19] But even given

12. University of Central Arkansas, "ChatGPT: What Is It?"

13. University of Central Arkansas, "ChatGPT: What Is It?"

14. University of Central Arkansas, "ChatGPT: What Is It?"

15. Truly, "5 Amazing Things People Have."

16. For a brief look at the mind-boggling capabilities of quantum computing, watch the *60 Minutes* news piece, "Companies, Countries Battle to Develop."

17. A qubit stands for "quantum bits." Twenty qubits are a million times more powerful than a classical computer. 60 Minutes, "Companies, Countries Battle to Develop."

18. Rutter and Mintz, "ChatGPT."

19. See more from Professor Steven Mintz at https://stevenmintz.substack.com/. Professor Mintz, who is a distinguished historian and professor at the University of Texas at Austin, argues that AI is removing our humanity. He argues for the reinstitution of the Socratic dialogue, oral tradition, and live interaction to save modern education.

his discretions, Professor Mintz has included ChatGPT in some projects. He has his students write a five-hundred-word essay by first prompting an input into ChatGPT, implementing the automated essay, but then building upon the essay with the input created by NI, before correcting, revising, and adding to the work of AI.

Multiple schools and universities have implemented safeguards that will hopefully detect the unauthorized use of AI for papers and essays through Turnitin and other plagiarism detectors. Susan D'Agostino maintains that

> when humans write, they leave subtle signatures that hint at the prose's fleshy, brainy organs. Their word and phrase choices are more varied than those selected by machines that write. Human writers also draw from short- and long-term memories that recall a range of lived experiences and inform personal writing styles.[20]

The ideas of D'Agostino are worth considering. AI technology cannot express the lived experiences of NI.[21] But even if AI could formulate the contents of a person's experiences, the personal eyewitness testimony of NI agents is invaluable and should not be replaced by AI or any other innovation.

Defining Plagiarism

Plagiarism is the unauthorized use of another person's intellectual property to claim and present it as one's own work. Oxford University further holds that "all published and unpublished material, whether in manuscript, printed or electronic form, is covered under this definition, as is the use of material generated wholly or in part through the use of artificial intelligence (save when the use of AI for assessment has received prior authorization)."[22] Notice the statement concerning the use of AI. Many schools have adopted similar policies.

Should the use of AI for written projects be considered plagiarism? Well, it depends on how the technology is used. If the written material developed by AI is used completely unadulterated and claimed to be the intellectual property of an NI agent, then the person in question is indubitably

20. D'Agostino, "AI Writing Detection," para. 1.
21. At least as of the time of this writing.
22. Oxford University, "Plagiarism," para. 2.

guilty of plagiarism. In said case, the NI agent claims something as one's own when it originated from AI. From my perspective, I think the deception involved in taking something developed by AI and claiming it as one's own is obvious. Nevertheless, a few additional reasons why this is the case will be addressed later in the chapter. But first, let's consider the value of truth and honesty.

THE VIRTUES OF TRUTH AND HONESTY (VIRTUE ETHICS)

Theologically speaking, Christians should especially concern themselves with the ethical virtues of truth and honesty. In the book of Exodus, God was revealed as the "Lord—the Lord is a compassionate and gracious God, slow in anger and abounding in faithful love and truth" (Exod 34:6).[23] Those who commit themselves as disciples of the Lord would especially be concerned with maintaining a high quality of character in their work. Unfortunately, this is not always the case. When I started teaching at a Christian college, I was told by other professors in the program that students often were inclined to plagiarize material when they ran out of time. Out of desperation, some will lessen their standards and will be tempted to plagiarize material simply to get their work submitted in time. But even in these circumstances, the believer must ask oneself if they are willing to sacrifice their spiritual fidelity simply in exchange for their own procrastination.

As a believer, the Christian should be committed to truth and honesty. How could the believer expect a skeptic to accept their claims of bearing witness to the miraculous and the life-changing power of Christ if the Christian is otherwise untrustworthy? Quite simply, they shouldn't. Consider the high value found in truth and honesty.

The Virtue of Truth in Writing (Using the Philosophy of Thomas Aquinas)

Truthfulness is an important quality for any believer to hold. Truth is best understood as I noted in a previous publication: "*Truth is what exists in*

23. Unless otherwise noted, all Scripture quoted in this chapter is taken from the Christian Standard Bible (CSB).

reality."[24] Acknowledging truth from fiction often originates from a spirit of wisdom and discernment. Another term to describe this quality would be prudence.[25] Norman Geisler reflects on prudence by noting that "prudence furnishes the right plan for immediate conduct,"[26] or "prudence is the *right reason of things to be done*."[27] Aquinas believed that prudence (wisdom) served as a gateway for other Christian virtues.[28] Of those habits and virtues that should be held in high esteem, truth is one of the highest. Aquinas held that when "anyone endowed with an art produces bad workmanship, this is not the work of that art, in fact, it is contrary to the art: even as when a man, while knowing the truth, lies, his works are not in accord with his knowledge, but contrary thereto."[29]

Considering the words of Aquinas, one must concede that the reckless use of generative AI to produce works as the product of an NI agent is dishonest to the core and does not portray honest, prudent behavior. Some people online—who shall remain nameless—claimed to have written books, whether whole or in part, with the use of AI generative apps. Yet the NI authors using AI stated that they would not identify AI as the originator of the work as they guided the process. However, it stuns me why anyone would use AI to write a book and claim it as one's own intellectual property. "Oh," some will say, "but I entered the prompts that guided the generative AI program." Entering prompts does not indicate that the contents of the work are one's own. On a Facebook post, Scott Klusendorf noted that not one word of his books was ghostwritten or generated by AI—never have and never will.[30] Klusendorf noted the importance of integrity in one's written documents.

Furthermore, why would someone want to buy a book from an author using AI generative apps? All someone needs to do is to enter the same prompts as the one who purportedly wrote the book. The practice is simply

24. Chilton, *Layman's Manual on Christian Apologetics*, 19.

25. *Merriam-Webster Dictionary* defines prudence as the "ability to govern and discipline oneself by the use of reason"; "sagacity or shrewdness in the management of affairs"; "skill and good judgment in the use of resources"; and "caution or circumspection as to danger or risk." *Merriam-Webster Dictionary*, "Prudence."

26. Geisler, *Thomas Aquinas*, 170.

27. Aquinas, *Summa Theologica* I–II.q.57.a4.

28. Aquinas, *Summa Theologica* II.a.2.ae; Geisler, *Thomas Aquinas*, 170.

29. Aquinas, *Summa Theologica* I–II.q.57.a.3.ad.1.

30. Scott Klusendorf's social media post, Mar. 9, 2024. Klusendorf is the president of Life Training Institute and is a contributing writer at the *Christian Research Journal*.

dishonest. The same goes for songs or movie scripts written by AI. As Aquinas noted, the so-called author knew whether they actually wrote the book, regardless of their claims. If a person's knowledge of an action does not match what occurred in reality, then the practice is deceptive.[31]

The Bible places a high value on truth as well. In the Old Testament, the term אֱמֶת (*emeth*) is commonly used to describe truth. *Emeth* speaks of factuality, validity, faithfulness, firmness, and reliability.[32] In Deut 13, the word *emeth* speaks of the factuality of a legal investigation. The text reads, "You are to inquire, investigate, and interrogate thoroughly. If the report turns out to be true (*emeth*) that this detestable act has been done among you, you must strike down the inhabitants of that city with the sword" (Deut 13:14–15).

Daniel used the word *emeth* to describe the truthfulness of the vision he received from God. He writes, "In the third year of Cyrus king of Persia, a message was revealed to Daniel, who was named Belteshazzar; and the message was true (*emeth*) and it concerned great conflict, but he understood the message and had an understanding of the vision" (Dan 10:1 NASB). Another example could be found when the king of Israel begged Micaiah to tell the truth (*emeth*) when prophesying. Additionally, the widow of Zarephath said to the prophet Elijah, "Now I know that you are a man of God, and that the word of the Lord in your mouth is truth (*emeth*)" (1 Kgs 17:24 NASB).

In the New Testament, the most common word used for truth is ἀλήθεια (*aletheia*). The word denotes three things: factuality, faithfulness/reliability, and reality.[33] Concerning factuality, the apostle Paul contrasts truth with falsehood, saying, "I speak the truth (*aletheia*) in Christ—I am not lying; my conscience testifies to me through the Holy Spirit" (Rom 9:1).

Regarding faithfulness and/or reliability, Paul again assists, as he writes, "Let God be true (*aletheia*), even though everyone is a liar" (Rom 3:4). Finally, Jesus used *aletheia* to speak of reality in several of his messages. For instance, Jesus taught that he was the true light (John 1:9) and said that the Father desires genuine worshipers, saying, "But an hour is coming, and now is here, when the true (*alethinos*) worshipers will worship the Father in Spirit and in truth (*aletheia*). Yes, the Father wants such people to worship

31. Furthermore, one would think that the so-called author would have no clue about the contents of the book if he or she is asked to speak about the book.

32. Ritzema, "Truth."

33. Ritzema, "Truth."

him. God is spirit, and those who worship him must worship in Spirit and in truth (*aletheia*)" (John 4:23–24).

In all the scriptural passages noted—which many others could be added—a heavy emphasis is on speaking about God in truth and living reliable lives. The believer is to be an ambassador of God. And what kind of ambassador would one be if they lied about the authenticity of their writings? While the apostle Paul used an amanuensis,[34] he would have been directly involved with the writing. It is not as if he would have given a mere prompt. The scribe would write what the apostle directed. He would have read back the passage, and the apostle would have shaped the document along with the scribe.

Now, advocates of AI would say, "That is what we are doing when we use AI. We give the prompts, and the generative program creates the document." Granted, there might be a few similarities. However, the primary difference lies in originality. The apostle would direct the wording and phrasing of the document. Admittedly, the scribe would provide his wording in key areas as the document was shaped. Yet the apostle was directly involved in the message. With generative writing apps, AI dictates the wording, phrasing, and information while the NI author remains passive. Thus, with the scribal process, both the author and scribe are active agents.

In stark contrast, the AI scribe is the active agent, whereas the NI author is passive in the generative writing activity. The two processes may seem similar at first glance, but they are distinctly different when considering the active role the author plays. With the former, the author maintains his voice. With the latter, the author loses her voice, which leads to a form of deception and dishonesty in the final product.[35] Such behaviors are not becoming of a child of God. This leads us to the virtue of honesty.

The Virtue of Honesty in Writing

What is God like? Does morality exist transcendently, or is it merely a matter of personal insight and opinion? While space will not permit a full

34. That is, a professional scribe.

35. It should also be noted that the author usually acknowledged the amanuensis when one was employed. Note that Romans identifies Paul as the author of the letter (Rom 1:1). However, Tertius is later identified as the amanuensis of the epistle (Rom 16:22). Colossians identifies Timothy as the likely amanuensis and Paul as the author (Col 1:1). In some epistles, like Galatians, the amanuensis may not be directly named. Yet Paul confirms that one was used (Gal 6:11).

treatment of the issue, all of us can justify our belief in good and evil. Nearly everyone would agree that it is morally good to help someone who is in need. On the other hand, nearly everyone would accept that the raping of young girls is morally evil. Moral apologists, such as David Baggett and Jerry Walls, support the view that the affinity between God's perfect goodness and omnibenevolence, variants of the cosmological and ontological arguments, and moral realism[36] all point to God's existence as an Anselmian God. The Anselmian God—first argued by Anselm of Canterbury (AD 1033–1109)—is the understanding that God exists as a Being who is "maximally perfect in every way, including morally."[37]

If we accept the concept of an Anselmian God,[38] then we ought to accept that we are obliged by moral obligations. Moral obligations are understood to be inescapable imperatives.[39] These moral obligations impact everyone since God is a necessary omnibenevolent Being. Nonetheless, those who wear the banner of a disciple of Christ are even more obliged to live morally. Of all the moral obligations we find in the pages of Scripture, honesty is held in the highest esteem, so much so that it made the Decalogue (i.e., the Ten Commandments). The ninth commandment admonishes people to live honest lives, saying, "Do not give false testimony against your neighbor" (Exod 20:16). Additionally, the eighth commandment states that a person should not steal (Exod 20:15). Let's consider these two commandments within the paradigm of unethical usages of ChatGPT.

First, consider the ninth commandment: "Do not give false testimony against your neighbor" (Exod 20:16). When a person uses ChatGPT to ghostwrite a paper, chapter, or book in their name, then the author is guilty of false advertising. The content of the book does not belong to them. Rather, the content belongs to the one who programmed ChatGPT to write the book. ChatGPT relies on data written by others. So, should the makers of ChatGPT then not receive a cut of the royalties from falsely advertised

36. Moral realism is the belief in the existence of "necessary moral truths, moral truths that couldn't be otherwise." That is, moral truths exist transcendently beyond the scope of personal opinion. Baggett and Walls, *Good God*, 52.

37. Otherwise known as the "God of the philosophers." Baggett and Walls, *Good God*, 51.

38. Sometimes called the "God of the philosophers." Baggett and Walls, *Good God*, 51.

39. "Moral obligations are no just rules or, worst, suggestions, like the rules of the road in Rome. Moral obligations are not mere options for us, even options supported by good reasons. They are thought to be *inescapable*." Baggett and Baggett, *Morals of the Story*, 136.

books? I would think so, especially when we consider the importance of copyrighting intellectual property. Additionally, the consumer is falsely led to believe that the book stems from the rationale of the one whose name is on the book. However, the author cannot assume credit for the content of the work because the content did not come from them. Can you imagine an author going on a speaking tour for a book pseudonymously written by an AI app? Can you imagine the Q&A after the speaking engagement?

The questioner to the author of an AI-written Christian book: "What did you mean on page 51 of your book when you said that you didn't think there were good reasons for believing in God?"

The author: "Oh, I definitely believe there are good reasons for believing in the existence of God."

The questioner: "But you wrote otherwise on page 51." The questioner then reads the paragraph to the author.

The author, stupefied, confesses that he did not write the book but used an AI app to write the book on his behalf. Disgruntled, the audience departs, and his book sales plummet after an audience member posts the interaction on YouTube.

Such a speaking engagement would result in a catastrophic disaster! Even if such an interaction didn't occur, in my estimation, one of the greatest problems using ChatGPT as an anonymous writer of papers, books, and plays is the deceptiveness of the practice. Simply put—we cannot claim intellectual ownership for things we did not write. Entering prompts is not the same as poring over a writing, critically thinking through different concepts, and carefully choosing the appropriate words to express oneself to the fullest.

Second, contemplate the meaning of the sixth commandment: "Do not steal" (Exod 20:13). The term *ganab* means to steal away, carry away, or to bring something by stealth.[40] Glen Martin reflects on the commandment, noting that stealing "included more than outright removal of another's property but also injury to another's possessions and fraudulent practices of any kind."[41] In the New Testament, the apostle Paul adds that the Spirit of God transforms a person to no longer steal. Rather, the believer should "do honest work with his own hands, so that he has something to share with anyone in need" (Eph 4:28).

40. Strong, "1589: *Ganab*."

41. Martin, *Exodus, Leviticus, Numbers*, 89.

Thinking about the spiritual temptation to use ChatGPT to take the easy way out, Jesus reminds us that Satan is the "father of lies" (John 8:44) and leads others to do likewise. God desires his people to live honestly and to be filled with truth and integrity in the inner parts of humanity (Ps 51:6). Therefore, any practice that involves laying claim to the authorship of material that did not originate from the author in question is essentially theft and breaks the sixth commandment.

Honesty is an honorable trait and is indicative of a person following the ways of God. Aquinas holds that a "thing may be said to be honest through being worthy of honor. . . . Therefore, properly speaking, honesty refers to the same thing as virtue."[42] Furthermore, honesty stems from God, who is the author of all things beautiful. Aquinas agrees with Dionysius, who wrote that God is the "cause of the harmony and clarity of the universe."[43] Dionysius the Areopagite (c. first-century AD) asserted that God is the author of "Divine Subsistence, Goodness; and because the Good, as essential Good, by Its Being, extends Its Goodness to all things that be."[44] And because God extends the virtue of honesty to all his creatures, therefore, honesty is useful and pleasing to those who promote it.[45] Honesty is a form of beauty, belonging to temperance, which addresses the beauty of the good and reason.[46]

As we have shown thus far, using generative writing apps such as ChatGPT to ghostwrite papers, chapters, books, songs, and plays while using a human creator's name as the author is dishonest, unethical, and plagiarizing. Theologically, the practice is unbecoming of a person who claims to have received the goodness of God. Biblically, God is the author of truth, whereas Satan is the father of lies, thus causing problems with the practice. Ethically, since an author essentially lies about the ownership of

42. Aquinas, *Summa Theologica* II–II.q.145.a.1.resp.

43. Dionysius, *Divine Names* 4.1. The book of Dionysius postdates the author by a few centuries. However, it is possible, if not likely, that the finished document stemmed from oral traditions and teachings from the author that was passed down until it was finally documented. External citations of the work have been discovered that predate the finished writing. Thus, some may argue that the inclusion of this book overrides the argument presented. Yet studies in oral traditions show that material can be passed down several generations without changing any core content. For more information on oral traditions, see Chilton, "Semitic Residue"; Bailey, "Informal Controlled Oral Tradition."

44. Dionysius, *Divine Names* 4.1.

45. Aquinas, *Summa Theologica* II–II.q.145.a3.resp.

46. Aquinas, *Summa Theologica* II–II.q.145.a4.resp.

the ideas presented, then deception is involved with the presentation of the generatively written document. Philosophically, God is an Anselmian God, existing necessarily as the source of all goodness, beauty, and truth. Literature should stem from original human ideas since humans are the recipients of God's goodness.

But all the above stems from the argument that authors claiming original works as their own that stemmed from generative apps like ChatGPT constitute plagiarism. Although the chapter has already given several good reasons to posit that it does, the remainder of the chapter will reveal practical reasons why the abuse of generative apps should be constituted as plagiarism, while also denoting the dangers involved with an overreliance on AI.

REASONS WHY THE ABUSE OF CHATGPT SHOULD BE CONSIDERED PLAGIARISM

Sergeant Joe Friday from the classic TV show *Dragnet* often had a tagline that transcended the show. He would often say, "All we want are the facts, ma'am." He did not need the fluff and extraneous details. Rather, he just wanted those facts that were essential to the case. While the ethical and philosophical matters are far from fluffy and extraneous, we have reached a point where we need to deal with the essential reasons why the unethical use of generative writing apps should be considered plagiarism. This list is far from exhaustive. Nevertheless, the chapter offers four justifications for why this position is held. As has already been explained, the section will use the abbreviation NI to reference natural intelligence (human users) and AI for artificial intelligence (automated apps).

Before peering into the reasons why the unethical use of generative writing apps like ChatGPT should be considered plagiarism, we should first mention the different kinds of plagiarism recognized by academia. While the types of plagiarism differ from one institution to the next, four are generally agreed upon by academia.

The first form of plagiarism is the easiest to detect—direct plagiarism. Direct plagiarism occurs when the writer transcribes the work of another word-for-word without ascribing credit to the source with quotation marks and a footnote or endnote.[47] For many schools, direct plagiarism is grounds for expulsion.

47. Office of the Dean of Students,"Common Types of Plagiarism."

The second form of plagiarism is known as self-plagiarism. This occurs when a writer submits parts of previous works without the authorization of one's professor. In professional writing environments, the writer often identifies if the material was previously published with notes that state, "Portions of this work were adapted from the previously published book or paper entitled __________."

The third form of plagiarism is called mosaic plagiarism. No, the title does not refer to Moses, but rather to a mosaic, which integrates various pieces and patches into floor and wall decorations to make a finished pattern. Sometimes this model is called "patch-writing."[48] The writer, in this case, borrows phrases and ideas from a source without citing the material. At times, the writer may change a word or two to paraphrase the material. The problem is that the material did not derive from the author's mind but rather from another resource.

Finally, the fourth form of plagiarism is called accidental plagiarism. As the name implies, accidental plagiarism is not intentional. Rather, the writer fails to cite their sources or even misquotes their sources. Bowdoin College states that accidental plagiarism happens when a "person neglects to cite their sources, or misquotes their sources, or unintentionally paraphrases a source by using similar words, groups of words, and/or sentence structure without attribution. This is a combination of Hybrid, Mashup, Aggregator, and Re-Tweet plagiarism."[49]

First, a NI writer is dishonest when they claim that the AI work is original to them. Not to belabor this point, but it should be recognized just how unethical this is. Plagiarism is understood to be deceptive because one person, let's call them NI1, claims that the work from another person, let's call them NI2, is their own. According to Harvard University, plagiarism is defined as follows:

> In academic writing, it is considered plagiarism to draw any idea or any language from someone else without adequately crediting that source in your paper. It doesn't matter whether the source is a published author, another student, a website without clear authorship, a website that sells academic papers, or any other person. Taking credit for anyone else's work is stealing, and it is

48. Office of the Dean of Students, "Common Types of Plagiarism," para. 4.
49. Office of the Dean of Students, "Common Types of Plagiarism," para. 5.

> unacceptable in all academic situations, whether you do it intentionally or by accident.[50]

If AI writes a document, then NI1 cannot claim the document flowed from the thoughts of NI1. The prompts do not dictate original thoughts. Say, for instance, NI1 asked the AI app to write about religious pluralism. AI may cite sources that speak on religious pluralism and how the philosophy accepts all religions as equally true. However, the information did not come from NI1 and, thereby, could not represent the original thoughts of the author. The information developed and written by the AI writing app could be said to represent the programming design of NI2. Thus, without giving proper credit, NI1 plagiarized both the AI writing app and the programming design of NI2. Noting the various forms of plagiarism noted by numerous universities and colleges, the unethical use of generative writing apps would fit at least three forms of plagiarism: direct, mosaic, and accidental.

The second reason the unethical use of generative writing apps should be considered plagiarism confronts one of the most common objections offered for its use. A few individuals have asked, "If you use Grammarly and Logos Bible Software, are you not guilty of using the same kind of technology for your papers, articles, and books?" Most assuredly not! The second reason why generative apps like ChatGPT should be considered plagiarism is that unethical usage would allow the app to write the material for them, whereas other apps, such as Grammarly and Logos Bible Software are used for research and fine-tuning of the finished document.

Given that many of our readers may not know what Logos and Grammarly are, let's take a few moments to discuss what these apps do. First, let us consider Logos Bible Software. Logos Bible Software is the gold-standard Bible app for biblical, theological, and philosophical scholars, students, and teachers of Christian studies. Logos Bible Software, based out of Bellingham, Washington, is a multifaceted resource that offers numerous digital books, commentaries, Bible translations, and multiple language tools in Greek, Hebrew, and Aramaic to assist the writer in their research. To my knowledge, Logos does not write anything for anyone. Rather, it assists in research by allowing the writer to examine thousands of resources with a simple search.[51] If generative apps are used in this fashion, then no ethical problems arise.

50. Harvard Guide to Using Sources, "What Constitutes Plagiarism?," para. 1.

51. As will be noted later in this chapter, the use of ChatGPT in this fashion is within

Also, Grammarly cannot be attributed to the same usage of generative writing apps due to the nature of its functionality. Grammarly is a tool that offers suggestions on writing style, including clarifying confusing statements and correcting typos. Thus, the difference is that the author has already written the document by the time Grammarly is employed, whereas generative writing apps write the document for the author. Granted, at the time of this writing, it is not known if Grammarly offers the same utilities as ChatGPT.[52] However, for the research practices of this author and those on the Bellator Christi writing team, Grammarly is used as an editorial writing aid, not a ghostwriter. Therefore, it is a categorical fallacy to ascribe the use of research apps like Logos Bible Software and editorial aids such as Grammarly to generative writing applications. In the former sense, the apps are used for research and editing. For the latter, the software is used to ghostwrite the document on the writer's behalf. The use of the former is legitimate in nearly all forms, whereas the use of the latter is unethical in all its iterations.

Third, the material offered on ChatGPT cannot be fully trusted without further research. Thus, the user may not have complete source material peering deeper into the material. Take an example of using ChatGPT to see where Aristotle wrote about the law of identity and logic. ChatGPT gave me a general book to investigate, but it never offered the reference in Aristotle's *Organon* where Aristotle wrote about such things. If a person blindly used ChatGPT to write one's papers, then the material would be unique to the app even when giving vague information. In one such case, the app offered a quote that it often attributed to Thomas Aquinas. However, the quote came from an unverified online author who offered a synopsis of what Aquinas said. No citations were offered. Thus, there was no way to validate that the words actually came from the pen of Aquinas. In this case, NI1 would have been guilty of accidental plagiarism, all because of blindly accepting what the AI software wrote.

Fourth, the NI user could potentially face legal consequences with published material using generative writing apps due to the unintentional plagiarism of already copyrighted material. Researchers have well documented that AI writing apps undergo memory lapses, often called short-term amnesia. That is not to say that the developers of the software won't

the boundaries of ethical usage and is recommended.

52. One should note that using Grammarly to rephrase paragraphs can lead to false positives on AI detectors like TurnItIn.

find a fix. They very well may. However, no one could ever guarantee that any automated application could ensure that the copyrighted material of others was not infringed with the material generated. If the author publishes the material, then the NI author could be charged with copyright infringement. The naysayer would say, "Yeah, but the NI user should check the material before publishing it." True. But even then, the NI user cannot be assured that what was written by the generative app was not borrowed, patch-written, or paraphrased from previously published material.

As intelligent as the human species is, I dare say that there is no human being alive who has comprehensive knowledge of all published material ever written. Consider that in a given year, it is estimated that 2 million books are self-published and an additional million books are released through a publisher.[53] That is not even considering that, according to a 2016 report by Google Books, some 134,021,533 total books were on record.[54] Providing that around 3 million books are published each year and we are eight years from the given total, then there must be 24 million more books to add to the total, not even including this work. Thus, the overall total of books in the storehouse of Google Books would be somewhere around 158,021,533 titles. For the NI user to guarantee that nothing was plagiarized, the writer would need to have comprehensive knowledge of all 158 million publications.

Remember, generative writing apps often draw from materials online, including resources that are in part available online. Simply put—there is no way that any human being alive could assure that the generative writing app did not draw from one of the 158 million titles available, and that's not even considering the numerous other works that may not be included in this collection.

Furthermore, recognize that this comes from a certified bibliophile (i.e., "booklover"). I would estimate that I have at least 2,500 paper books in my possession—and the total is likely much higher. When you count the e-books I own through Logos Bible Software and Kindle, the overall total of books in my possession likely skyrockets well beyond 4,000. While I have read most of the books in my library, I cannot guarantee that I could automatically detect if ChatGPT plagiarized the materials in my possession, much less those titles of which I am unaware. As much as it may pain many to hear, writing the old-fashioned way through research and original

53. Piersanti, "10 Awful Truths."

54. Panganiban, "How Many Books Have Ever."

writing by NI is the only way to ensure that the writer does not plagiarize the works of other writers—both NI and AI.

DANGERS OF AN OVERRELIANCE ON CHATGPT

Thus far, the chapter has offered reasons why the unethical use of generative writing apps should be considered plagiarism. But let's take a few moments to consider some inherent dangers that could come from an overreliance on AI technology. There are quite a few to take into consideration.

First, an overreliance on generative writing apps like ChatGPT can lead to a devolution of the human intellect. I was born in the '70s, meaning that I am part of Generation X. As such, when I was a child and into my teenage years, I had to memorize the phone numbers that were important for me to remember. To this day, my parents' home phone number easily comes to mind. It was not until I was in my twenties that I bought my first cell phone. Even then, I had one of the block phones that was far from one that you would carry in your pocket. Into my thirties, I had a flip phone. When the smartphones came out, I swore up and down that I would never purchase one of them. However, my wife and I observed that the phone company offered better deals with smartphones than the traditional flip phones. Smartphones store phone numbers with great ease, lessening the importance of one's memorization of phone numbers. However, now, I have noticed that it is much more difficult for me to memorize phone numbers than it was before I owned a smartphone. Muscle memory is a reality, and the less we use our ability to memorize, the worse we become memorizing information in general. At the time of this publication, medical research is already revealing cognitive decline in those who depend heavily on AI. Research indicates that individuals possess less critical thinking skills along with a decline in memory.[55]

Additionally, living in a time where information can be obtained with lightning speed, the patience and cognitive retention of most people have been greatly reduced. Neil Postman recognized that the attention spans of the American public had exponentially lessened from the 1800s. Postman recalled a series of debates that transpired between Stephen A. Douglas and Abraham Lincoln, the first of which occurred on Saturday, August 21, 1858, in Ottawa, Illinois.[56] Douglas spoke first for an hour, then Lincoln would

55. Chow, "ChatGPT May Be Eroding."

56. Postman, *Amusing Ourselves to Death*, 44.

take an hour and a half to respond.[57] Earlier, Douglas and Lincoln debated on October 16, 1854, in Peoria, Illinois. In this event, Douglas gave a three-hour address with great oratory skills. At 5:00 p.m., Lincoln requested that everyone return home for supper and return within an hour, because he would need at least three hours to respond. Everyone returned and listened with rapt attention.[58] These days, one is lucky to have people sit through a forty-minute sermon without getting fidgety, much less a three-hour talk. Additionally, listeners would have needed to have learned information about events, discussions, and legislation to understand the intricacies of Douglas's and Lincoln's oratorical addresses.[59]

Third, even though generative writing apps will grow more accurate with time, the app will still likely draw information from the internet. As such, the app will merely report the information it receives. However, it will not have the ability to determine whether the information is correct or not. The NI user will have to research to see whether the information is factually accurate. There may be others, though, that blindly accept the data the AI app affords.

A good example of this situation was found when my son and I typed in "socialism" in a ChatGPT app. ChatGPT noted the different opinions related to socialism and offered a working definition of the style of government. However, my son and I observed a noticeable slant toward socialism. Someone who blindly accepted the material from the app may be inclined to accept socialistic concepts. Does this sound too far-fetched? Well, it may not be as incredible as one might think.

Fourth, overreliance on ChatGPT is just another example of how our culture cultivates a celebration of laziness. St. Thomas Aquinas maintains that laziness flows from a person's fear of toiling too much, which ultimately leads to disgrace.[60] Picture if you will television shows from the '50s and '60s. Many of the ads pushed the latest technological advances in an attempt to make life easier. In many ways, the products did just that. Granted, most of us are thankful for technological advances such as enjoying a nice, air-conditioned home on a hot, summer day. It is one thing to appreciate the comforts that come with technology. It is quite another to become overly dependent on those advances.

57. Postman, *Amusing Ourselves to Death*, 44.

58. Postman, *Amusing Ourselves to Death*, 44.

59. Postman, *Amusing Ourselves to Death*, 44–50.

60. Aquinas, *Summa Theologica* I–II.q.41.a4.resp.

Consider this: Years ago, the pastor was expected to be the most educated person in the entire community. However, today, in some rural locales, spirituality is equated to unpreparedness, speaking with a steep regional dialect, and making inaccurate claims in an attempt to seem more spiritual. A recent example could be seen in a video of a pompous fundamentalist preacher making its rounds on social media. The heavyset preacher, adorned with suit and tie, proudly said, "I believe the King James Bible is the Word of God, every word of it." Off-screen, several congregants can be heard laughing before egging on the preacher with a steep Southern-accented, "Amen!" Filled with added courage due to his congregational cheerleaders, much like a child who feels emboldened by his parent's laughter, the preacher continues by making a bold claim, saying, "I can take this book and correct the Greek." Again, the congregant serves as the pastor's cheerleader as he is heard laughing and saying, "Oh, yeah! Ha ha!" The preacher is then seen tugging his coat down with both hands to further brag about his emboldened claim.[61]

The level of absurdity behind this assertion is profound. The Chicago Statement on Biblical Inerrancy (CSBI)—a declarative compilation of propositions pertaining to the Bible's inspiration and inerrancy—acknowledges that the original biblical manuscripts in their respective languages serve as the infallible, inerrant word of God, not a man-made translation. The CSBI affirms that the inspiration of Scripture "applies only to the autographic text of Scripture, which in the providence of God can be ascertained from available manuscripts with great accuracy."[62] Given that the English language did not come about until AD 1000, this places the earliest possible translation of Scripture some 900 years after the Bible was completed. Thus, if God inspired the writers of Scripture, how could they have written the revelation of God into a language that had not yet been invented? Such a notion is absurd.

With this in mind, why would the preacher and congregant be so willing to embrace a historical absurdity? This only shows the level of intellectual laziness that has crept into the modern church, which in turn flows

61. It was later learned that the pastor in question is the controversial evangelist Mark McGaughey of Alabama. Wildsmith, "Dangerous KJV Only."

62. Defending Inerrancy, "Chicago Statement on Biblical Inerrancy," art. 10. The Evangelical Theological Society's doctrinal basis is termed as follows: "The Bible alone, and the Bible in its entirety, is the Word of God written as inerrant in the autographs. God is a Trinity, Father, Son, and Holy Spirit, each an uncreated person, one in essence, equal in power and glory." Evangelical Theological Society, "Preface."

from the intellectual laziness adopted by the culture at large. Unfortunately, the church is not immune to the influence of modern culture.

Fifth, an overreliance on artificial intelligence could potentially lead to the further degradation of human creativity. When human beings rely on technology to write and produce material for them, the greatest tragedy of all is the impact it holds on human creativity. What is the beauty found in an image artificially produced rather than one that holds the emotions of its creator? Considering music, a song is much more impactful if one knows the meaning behind the composition.

For instance, who could forget the deep meaning behind Horatio Spafford's classic hymn "It Is Well With My Soul." Spafford was an American lawyer who lived in the 1800s. Spafford, a successful businessman, eventually faced trials and hardships to the level of the biblical Job. Spafford lost his four-year-old son to scarlet fever and lost several properties in the Great Chicago Fire of 1873, only to discover that his wife and daughters were involved in a fatal sinking of their ship in the Atlantic. As he traveled to the spot where his wife and daughters drowned in the Atlantic, Spafford wrote the popular hymn "It is Well With My Soul."[63] Spafford did not imply that he did not mourn the loss of his family and material goods. Rather, he proclaimed that even through the darkest moments of life, he would still trust in the sovereignty of God.

AI cannot replicate human emotions and soulish features since it is not a human being. It is for that reason that Tennessee governor Bill Lee signed legislation on March 21, 2025, that would protect songwriters, performers, and other professionals in the music industry against the dangers of artificial intelligence.[64] Nashville is the birthplace of country music, and the city has also become the birthplace of human creativity protection.

A sixth potential challenge with an overdependence on AI stems from exacerbated corporate expectations. Already, many employees feel overworked, overstressed, underpaid, and feel underappreciated. Some may contend that the integration of AI into the workforce could alleviate certain responsibilities. And to a degree, that could be true. But if corporations abuse the introduction of AI into the workforce, employers could potentially expect even more from employees who already feel pushed to the edge of desperation.

63. Wetherington, "What Is the Meaning Behind?"

64. Associated Press, "Tennessee Becomes First State."

Seventh, we must face the real possibility that the power grid could go down. If that occurs, how would humanity function if they have become so dependent on AI that they are no longer able to think for themselves? I remember helping my grandparents with canning food from the garden so that the vegetables and fruit could be enjoyed in the winter months. Canning food is becoming a lost art. The more humanity depends on technology, the less self-reliant humanity becomes.

Granted, we are not talking about gardening. But in many senses, we are talking about something even bigger—the ability of human beings to think, contemplate, and research. The more society depends on technology, the dumber we become. Earlier, I had mentioned the decreased ability to remember phone numbers now that I have a smartphone to store them. I am far from the only one experiencing this phenomenon. Many other local people have expressed the same problem. One lady told me that she had memorized her parents' phone number, along with her siblings, cousins, neighbors, and those of local businesses. Now, she said that she can barely remember her own.

Exacerbating this problem is the degradation of the modern educational system. In many circles, societal opinions replace historical facts. Books and movies that may contain certain problems have been canceled. Granted, I am not advocating that people endorse Hitler's *Mein Kampf* or the racist innuendos of *Gone with the Wind*. Yet these works only highlight the problems that stem from racist and fascist thinking. Rather than eliminating these works, people should be educated about them and the problems found therein. But that requires critical thinking skills. Additionally, many youths are not trained in how to write in cursive any longer. If technology crashes, the way you could cripple a society is to write messages in cursive where increasing amounts of individuals could never read what was communicated. All being said, if we further create a mode of dependency upon technology without the ability to evaluate, assess, diagnose, and make decisions, we will have not made a generation of future leaders. Rather, we would have merely made a generation of lemmings, willing to follow every ideological wind that blows by them. The image of humanity cast as floating globs of goo in the popular Disney movie *Wall-E* is something that is not beyond the realm of possibility.

APPROPRIATE USE AND BENEFITS OF CHATGPT

Up to this point, this chapter has offered reasons why human beings should not become overly dependent on generative writing apps like ChatGPT. You might think that I am something of a "negative Nancy" or a modern adaptation of Eeyore from the *Winnie the Pooh* series, seeing everything from an emotionally distressed platform. However, that assessment would be incorrect because I am not against technology, and I am really not against ChatGPT. It may surprise the reader to find that I have used ChatGPT for research and gathering resources for study. Now, before you charge me with hypocrisy, let the reader understand that to this point, I have argued for the responsible use of generative writing apps, of which ChatGPT is an example. Abuse of these apps is problematic, if not downright dangerous. However, that does not preclude that one should avoid ChatGPT and writing apps altogether. Before concluding this chapter, I would like to present five ways that ChatGPT and similar writing apps can be beneficial.

First, ChatGPT can help jump-start ideas. For anyone who has taught a lesson or delivered a message, you know that getting started is the most difficult component of the task. Once you have the thesis and outline in mind, the rest comes fairly easily. ChatGPT and generative writing apps can benefit a pastor, researcher, teacher, and student by gauging ideas, counterpoints, and possible trajectories that the lesson, sermon, or paper could follow. Using ChatGPT in this fashion assists the human agent to think through ideas and theories, and even consider possible options that would not be contemplated otherwise. In the end, the human agent may not adopt all the possible options given by AI. ChatGPT merely serves as an electronic tutor in this case.

Second, comparable to the first point, ChatGPT and generative writing apps may serve useful in assisting a person with research. When used in this fashion, ChatGPT can serve alongside Logos Bible Software and other libraries as a powerful research tool. Think of ChatGPT as a library cataloging system in this situation, only greatly enhanced. Like Logos Bible Software, AI can peruse the various books available on a topic. But unlike Logos Bible Software and similar apps, ChatGPT has all online resources at its disposal, both articles and books alike. When professors advocate for ChatGPT, it is largely for the app's great prowess as a research aid.

Third, I found another tremendous benefit of ChatGPT in my readings through extensive, heavy writings.[65] ChatGPT can be beneficial in outlining books and explaining difficult concepts. I have been reading through Thomas Aquinas's *Summa Theologica.* Some parts of Aquinas's work were more difficult than others. Not having access to a lot of Thomistic scholars, and to keep from bugging those that I did know, ChatGPT served as an invaluable resource to help me through the trickier parts of Aquinas's massive work.

Fourth, in collaboration with the previous point, ChatGPT can assist with sorting data. As noted, ChatGPT can help one focus on the more important details of a philosophical problem, rather than run endless rabbit trails on sidebar issues. For the busy pastor and/or teacher, ChatGPT could prove invaluable in outlining certain textbooks, especially when preparing lessons. According to every personality test I have ever taken, I have the mindset of a thorough, scholarly perfectionist—INTJ according to Myers-Brigg, yellow according to the MBS leadership assessment, and EI/CT on the Big Five. Because of that tendency, I often add too many details and too much information to a presentation. ChatGPT can be beneficial for people like me to focus on the essentials rather than overloading people with needless details.[66]

Fifth and finally, if ChatGPT is eventually connected with quantum computing, the app can aid in solving complex problems. The potential computing power of quantum computers is beyond comprehension. Experts estimate that quantum computers will be millions of times faster than modern computers today. Physicist Michio Kaku projects that the advent of quantum computers will turn everything upside down.[67] Kaku envisions that quantum computers will allow chemists to run chemistry trials without having to use chemicals due to the advanced simulations that the processors will be able to conduct. If this kind of computing power were added to ChatGPT, the possibilities for solving complex problems would be endless.[68]

65. Here, I am speaking of my reading through Thomas Aquinas's *Summa Theologica*, as noted in this chapter. However, I have also found benefits in outlining books of the Bible to prepare for Bible studies. Because of time constraints, ChatGPT was used along with Logos Bible Software to help me prepare for the Bible study in Galatians on the *Bellator Christi Podcast*, which aired the winter of 2024.

66. Some may even say that I am guilty of that problem in this chapter. Wink, wink.

67. Leith, "Everything Is Going to Be."

68. See also, Kaku, *Quantum Supremacy*.

CONCLUSION

At first glance, you may think that this chapter is polemical and casts technology in a very bad light. However, that is neither the intent nor the emphasis of this chapter. I am very much pro-technology and for any advancement that will benefit society as a whole. Generative writing apps are not bad. They do offer benefits to the researcher and/or writer. The problem stems from when a person, culture, or society relies so much on generative writing apps, or any technological advancement for that matter, to the point that the user can no longer critically think through ideas, distinguish truth from fantasy, or understand right from wrong.

As one who loves Marvel and DC comics, I am reminded of the words that Uncle Ben spoke to Peter Parker when he knew about Peter's newfound powers as Spiderman, saying, "With great power comes great responsibility."[69] The same holds true with generative writing apps. Artificial intelligence in general is largely amoral. It's neither good nor bad. Rather, how human beings use technology is what matters. The same holds true for anything in life. As the book of Proverbs advises, "If you find honey, eat only what you need; otherwise, you'll get sick from it and vomit" (Prov 25:16). As AI becomes more commonplace in popular parlance and ways of living, humanity may find that AI is like the metaphorical honey of Proverbs. But like honey, we only need to use it for what we need; otherwise, we may find that we vomit from the egregious complications that flow from an unhealthy dependency on technology.

BIBLIOGRAPHY

60 Minutes. "Companies, Countries Battle to Develop Quantum Computers." Dec. 4, 2023. YouTube video, 13:24. https://www.youtube.com/watch?v=K4ssT6Dzmnw.

Associated Press. "Tennessee Becomes First State to Pass a Law Protecting Musicians Against AI." CBS News, Mar. 21, 2024. https://www.cbsnews.com/news/tennessee-becomes-first-state-to-protect-musicians-and-other-artists-against-ai/.

Aquinas, Thomas. *Summa Theologica*. Translated by the Fathers of the English Dominican Province. London: Burns Oates & Washbourne, 1920.

Baggett, David, and Jerry L. Walls. *Good God: The Theistic Foundations of Morality*. Oxford: Oxford University Press, 2011.

Baggett, David, and Marybeth Baggett. *The Morals of the Story: Good News About a Good God*. Grand Rapids: IVP Academic, 2018.

69. The phrase is originally attributed to French author Voltaire.

Bailey, Kenneth E. "Informal Controlled Oral Tradition and the Synoptic Gospel." *Asia Journal of Theology* 5 (1991) 34–54.

Barry, John D., et al., eds. *The Lexham Bible Dictionary.* Bellingham, WA: Lexham, 2016. Logos Bible Software.

Chilton, Brian G. *The Layman's Manual on Christian Apologetics: Bridging the Essentials of Apologetics from the Ivory Tower to the Everyday Christian.* Eugene, OR: Resource, 2019.

Chilton, Brian Gray. "Semitic Residue: Semitic Traits that Indicate Early Source Material Behind the Gospel of Matthew." PhD diss., Rawlings School of Divinity, 2022. https://digitalcommons.liberty.edu/doctoral/3874.

Chow, Andrew R. "ChatGPT May Be Eroding Critical Thinking Skills, According to a New MIT Study." *Time*, Nov. 13, 2025. https://time.com/7295195/ai-chatgpt-google-learning-school/.

D'Agostino, Susan. "AI Writing Detection: A Losing Battle Worth Fighting." Inside Higher Ed, Jan. 19, 2023. https://www.insidehighered.com/news/2023/01/20/academics-work-detect-chatgpt-and-other-ai-writing.

Defending Inerrancy. "Chicago Statement on Biblical Inerrancy." https://defendinginerrancy.com/chicago-statements/.

Dionysius. *The Divine Names* 4.1. Transcribed by Roger Pearse, 2004. https://www.tertullian.org/fathers/areopagite_03_divine_names.htm#c4.

Evangelical Theological Society. "Preface." *Journal of the Evangelical Theological Society* 66.4 (2023).

Geisler, Norman L. *Thomas Aquinas: An Evangelical Appraisal.* Eugene, OR: Wipf & Stock, 1991.

Harvard Guide to Using Sources. "What Constitutes Plagiarism?" Harvard University. https://usingsources.fas.harvard.edu/what-constitutes-plagiarism-0.

Henson, Brea. "Types of Plagiarism." University of North Texas University Libraries, Aug. 9, 2023. https://guides.library.unt.edu/plagiarism/types.

Kaku, Michio. *Quantum Supremacy: How the Quantum Computer Revolution Will Change Everything.* New York: Doubleday, 2023.

Kreeft, Peter. *Socratic Logic.* South Bend, IN: St. Augustine's, 2014.

Leith, Sam. "'Everything Is Going to Be Turned Upside Down': Michio Kaku on the New World of Quantum Computing." *Spectator*, Apr. 29, 2023. https://spectator.com/article/everything-is-going-to-be-turned-upside-down-michio-kaku-on-the-new-world-of-quantum-computing/?edition=us.

Martin, Glen S. *Exodus, Leviticus, Numbers.* Holman Old Testament Commentary. Edited by Max Anders. Nashville: B&H, 2002.

Merriam-Webster Dictionary. "Prudence." https://www.merriam-webster.com/dictionary/prudence.

Michaels, Nikki. "15 AI Writing and Content Creation Tools." Shorthand. https://shorthand.com/the-craft/ai-writing-tools/index.html#.

Office of the Dean of Students. "The Common Types of Plagiarism." Bowdoin College. https://www.bowdoin.edu/dean-of-students/conduct-review-board/academic-honesty-and-plagiarism/common-types-of-plagiarism.html.

Oxford University. "Plagiarism: Information About What Plagiarism Is, and How You Can Avoid It." https://www.ox.ac.uk/students/academic/guidance/skills/plagiarism.

Panganiban, Roma. "How Many Books Have Ever Been Published." Mental Floss, Sept. 9, 2016. https://www.mentalfloss.com/article/85305/how-many-books-have-ever-been-published.

Piersanti, Steven. "The 10 Awful Truths About Book Publishing." Berrett-Koehler Publishers, Mar. 1, 2023. https://ideas.bkconnection.com/10-awful-truths-about-publishing.

Postman, Neil. *Amusing Ourselves to Death: Public Discourse in an Age of Show Business.* New York: Penguin, 1986.

Ritzema, Elliot. "Truth." *Lexham Bible Dictionary*. Logos Bible Software.

Rutter, Michael Patrick, and Steven Mintz. "ChatGPT: Threat or Menace?: Are Fears About Generative AI Warranted?" Inside Higher Ed, Jan. 15, 2023. https://www.insidehighered.com/opinion/columns/higher-ed-gamma/2023/01/15/chatgpt-threat-or-menace.

Stanton, Andrew, dir. *WALL-E*. Burbank, CA: Walt Disney Studios Motion Pictures, 2008.

Strong, James. *Enhanced Strong's Lexicon*. Ontario: Woodside Bible Fellowship, 1995. Logos Bible Software.

Truly, Alan. "5 Amazing Things People Have Already Done with ChatGPT." Digital Trends, Dec. 29, 2022. https://www.digitaltrends.com/computing/5-amazing-things-with-chatgpt/.

University of Central Arkansas. "ChatGPT: What Is It?" https://uca.edu/cetal/chat-gpt/.

Webb, Jack, dir. *Dragnet*. Season 2, episode 27, "The Big Lease." Written by James E. Moser. Aired May 14, 1953, on NBC.

Wetherington, Halie. "What Is the Meaning Behind the Song 'It Is Well with My Soul'?" ECB Publishing, Inc., July 12, 2022. https://ecbpublishing.com/what-is-the-meaning-behind-the-song-it-is-well-with-my-soul/.

Wildsmith, Tim. "Dangerous KJV Only." Sept. 24, 2014. YouTube video, 00:59. https://www.youtube.com/shorts/XKJoP3ed_yQ.

4

Stewarding Cognitive Liberty

A Call to Freedom from Mental Enslavement

Brian G. Chilton, PhD

Country musician Martina McBride popularized the song "Independence Day." The song tells the story of an abused woman who finds the strength to leave her abusive husband. The chorus sings, "Let freedom ring, let the white doves sing. Let the whole world know that today is a day of reckoning. Let the weak be strong, let the right be wrong. Roll the stone away, let the guilty pay, it's Independence Day!!!"[1] McBride's song of triumph of freedom over abuse won numerous awards, including the Best Video of the Year award in 1994, the Best Country Vocal Performance by a female and Best Country Song at the Grammys in 1995, and the Country Music Association's 1995 Song of the Year.

As I prepared to write this chapter, I tried my own rendition of "Independence Day." My wife looked at me unimpressed and said sarcastically, "You're no Martina." She was absolutely right! There are very few people who have the voice of Martina, but her emphasis on liberty is important in the new AI era. As we contemplate stewarding AI in a responsible fashion, we must consider the importance of human cognitive liberty.

As we analyze the potential impact that artificial intelligence (AI) could have on humanity, we must consider the lack of freedoms that *could*

1. Peters, "Independence Day."

come from the technology as it is implemented into everyday life. Although many sensors today are created to help individuals, we should consider the unintended consequences that may surface. One possibility could be cognitive enslavement stemming from the use of sensors, particularly those that are postulated to be inserted into the brain. Some specialists claim that AI-integrated sensors would make life even easier than before, as the technology could allow someone to make a phone call by merely thinking it.

Does this sound too far-fetched to be true? Think again. In 2024—the year that this chapter was compiled—Elon Musk and his team of engineers and surgeons successfully implanted a chip into the brain of a willing participant.[2] The sensor was implanted in the part of the brain that governs motor control. The goal was that the person would be connected to a computer and move the cursor by the mind alone. And initial tests have been successful, although there have been a few glitches along the way.[3]

Given the direction that society seems to be heading with the integration of AI and the biological aspects of human beings, it behooves us to consider the potential hindrances that could come to the mental freedom of the human soul. This chapter will contend that because of the *imago Dei*, human beings have the unalienable right to their own mental and cognitive freedoms. Permanent implanted technologies such as brain sensors could bring about a form of cognitive enslavement to AI, resulting in an unhealthy dependence on the technology, as well as the loss of privacy of one's mentality—that is, the loss of freedom to entertain one's own thoughts without someone else intruding upon them. If left unrestrained, such technologies could lead to abuse.

WHAT'S SO SERIOUS ABOUT BRAIN SENSORS?

Earlier, we briefly introduced the concept of brain sensors. We must ask ourselves, "Are brain sensors really all that bad?" Well, yes and no. On the positive side, brain sensors have afforded disabled persons the opportunity to interact with others in ways that they would not have been able to otherwise. For instance, researchers have connected quadriplegics to technologies that allow the person to move a cursor with merely their mind alone. In 2018,

2. Sriram and Ghosh, "Elon Musk's Neuralink Implants."

3. The sensor's sensitivity to the neurons of the volunteer's brain had to be increased. Golgowski, "Neuralink Reveals Issues."

> BrainGate, a collaboration between Brown University's Carney Institute for Brain Science, the Providence Veterans Affairs Medical Center (PVAMC), Massachusetts General Hospital (MGH) and Stanford University published research in PLOS ONE describing a successful implanted brain-computer interface (BCI). The technology allowed individuals with quadriplegia to operate electronic devices using thoughts.
>
> Three patients with quadriplegia were implanted with the BrainGate BCI, a sensor about the size of a baby aspirin. It can detect signals in the motor cortex. These were decoded and routed to a Bluetooth device that acts as a wireless mouse. They then used the mouse to surf the web, send emails, and stream audio/video. One participant used the device to play Beethoven's "Ode to Joy" on a digital piano.
>
> Senior author and Stanford neurosurgeon Jaimie Henderson told Forbes, "For years, the BrainGate collaboration has been working to develop the neuroscience and neuroengineering know-how to enable people who have lost motor abilities to control external devices just by thinking about the movement of their own arm or hand. In this study, we've harnessed the know-how to restore people's ability to control the exact same everyday technologies they were using before the onset of their illnesses."[4]

As noted, Elon Musk's Neuralink along with Mark Zuckerberg's Building 8 are also experimenting with the technology.

This technology creates many fascinating and, in some cases, frightening possibilities. Additionally, the concept of telepathy and telekinesis aren't as far-fetched as one might think. With the implementation of sensors, the patients are telepathically manipulating devices to evoke a telekinetic response. Could the mind do this alone? It seems that it is at least possible.

Granted, institutions like BrainGate should be applauded because they are giving new life to many who have experienced great loss. Nevertheless, the more pressing and concerning issue at hand does not involve the research by BrainGate to help people. Rather, the more concerning matter involves Neuralink and Building 8. Why would a social media mogul need access to a person's mentality? Furthermore, outside of assisting quadriplegics and others suffering from physical impairments, what need is there to implant chips into the human brain to use with phones and computers?

There are two major enslavements that implanted brain sensors could cause for people. First, if businesses and corporations had access to

4. Terry, "BrainGate's Technology," para. 1–4.

a person's thoughts, then a person could potentially lose their position for simply thinking something that goes against the company's stance. Imagine a world where tycoons control employees with technological devices that restrict any negativity on the employee's part. If an employee was not engaged in their work, the supervisor would have access to their mental production.

Again, this may sound far-fetched, but that is far from the case. In China, teachers are using headbands with sensors created by a Massachusetts company to gauge each student's learning, attentiveness, and mental performance.[5] The research is fraught with problems at the outset.[6] Nonetheless, the kind of mental control that seemingly derives from a dystopian sci-fi novel is very real and is being used as we speak. If this technology was used in manufacturing, or other businesses, an already stressed workforce would have even greater reasons to feel under the gun. Because their performance would not only be measured by physical production, but their cognitive adherence to the corporation and/or mental attentiveness would be gauged as well. Therein, people would lose their God-given right to their own mind.

Second, people run the risk of being even further enslaved to technology if they have complete mental dependence on said technologies due to their mental connection to the internet and their cell phones. A little later in the chapter, I will offer some medical research that shows the danger of children using technology too close to bedtime. As you will see, it is not healthy for people to have too much screen time near bedtime routines. Yet, how would that look if a person is implanted with technology that never shuts off? Theoretically, it is possible that a person could receive spam calls at all hours of the night without the ability to turn off the ring tone in their head. Such a scenario could drive one mad! We'll touch more on the inherent overdependence of such technology in a few moments. But first, we need to delve into a little philosophy to ask whether people genuinely have conscious cognitive freedom in the first place.

ARE CONSCIOUS BEINGS FREE? IS CONSCIOUSNESS SEPARATE FROM THE MATERIAL WORLD?

One of the questions that must be considered is whether human beings are consciously free in the first place. In other words, are human beings

5. Wexler, "Mind Control in China's Classrooms."
6. Wexler, "Mind Control in China's Classrooms."

constrained to a deterministic world from which no one could theoretically break free? Or are human beings consciously free to choose x versus y without outside interference?[7] To consider this perspective, let's consider some biblical and philosophical reasons to believe that humans maintain at least some sense of cognitive freedom.

Biblical Defense for Cognitive Freedom

The Bible not only states that people have an immaterial soul, but it also implies that we do have a sense of cognitive freedom. Concerning the former, Jesus exhorts his disciples to not fear those who can kill the body but not the soul, rather fear God who is able to destroy both soul and body in hell (Matt 10:28).[8] Paul also states the following:

> For we know that if our earthly tent we live in is destroyed, we
> have a building from God, an eternal dwelling in the heavens, not
> made with hands. 2 Indeed, we groan in this tent, desiring to put
> on our heavenly dwelling, 3 since, when we are clothed, we will
> not be found naked. 4 Indeed, we groan while we are in this tent,
> burdened as we are, because we do not want to be unclothed but
> clothed, so that mortality may be swallowed up by life. 5 Now the
> one who prepared us for this very purpose is God, who gave us the
> Spirit as a down payment.
>
> 6 So we are always confident and know that while we are at home
> in the body we are away from the Lord. 7 For we walk by faith,
> not by sight. 8 In fact, we are confident, and we would prefer to
> be away from the body and at home with the Lord. 9 Therefore,
> whether we are at home or away, we make it our aim to be pleas-
> ing to him. 10 For we must all appear before the judgment seat
> of Christ, so that each may be repaid for what he has done in the
> body, whether good or evil. (2 Cor 5:1–10)[9]

Additionally, the Bible states that the immaterial soul returns to God after one's death (Luke 16:19–23, 23:39–43). It also notes that the soul animates

7. This view is otherwise known as libertarian free will.

8. Some may think that this passage defends the temporality of hell, but there are a vast number of Scriptures that speak of hell as being an eternal place. Yet, that topic is not warranted in this discussion.

9. Unless otherwise noted, all quoted Scripture quoted in this chapter comes from the Christian Standard Bible (CSB).

the body (Luke 16:19–31; 1 Kgs 17:19–23), and that the soul remains active between a person's death and final resurrection (Eccl 12:5–7; Matt 17:1–3).[10] Thus, a strong case can be made for the immateriality of the soul and its immortal existence beyond the scope of death. But what does the Bible say about the soul's cognitive liberty?

Deuteronomy 30 states that a person has the cognitive freedom to choose life or death, God's blessings or curses (Deut 30:19). Moses then appeals to his listeners to choose the life found in God and his blessings rather than going down the route of death and curses (Deut 30:20). You could even make the case that the entire law of God is based upon a person's free will to choose the ways of Yahweh as opposed to the pagan gods of the world. A good case has been made that the ten plagues in the book of Exodus was God's appeal for the Hebrews and Egyptians to leave the gods of Egyptian culture and to follow Yahweh—the true God—instead.[11]

In the Gospel of John, the apostle states that God gave all who willfully believed in his name the right to become children of God (John 1:12–13). Jesus later states that if a person's desire was to live out God's will, then the person would know that his teaching was from God (John 7:17). Thus, this does not preclude God's working in a person's life and certainly does not endorse a form of Pelagianism.[12] However, for our purposes, Jesus merely shows that a person has the cognitive liberty to listen to God or reject what he says.

Finally, the apostle Paul speaks of a person's cognitive freedom to choose one way or another. To the Galatian church, he taught about the believer's liberty. Even still, he exhorted the Galatians not to abuse that freedom as an opportunity to serve the flesh, rather they should lovingly serve one another (Gal 5:13). He also states that a person will eventually reap the harvest of the crop they sowed (Gal 6:7), meaning that a person's choices have consequences.

Granted, theologically speaking, we cannot ignore the doctrine of predestination and God's free exercise of his will. Nonetheless, given the expressions of freedom, I would suggest a form of compatibilism when balancing human freedom and divine predestination. Such compatibilist notions are found in Thomism, Molinism, and even some lighter versions of Calvinism—such as one would find with the theological moorings of the late Norman Geisler. Regardless of which route one takes, it would be

10. Theologians often call this period the intermediate state.

11. Stuart, *Exodus*, 186–319.

12. The idea that a person can save oneself without the assistance of God.

advisable to eschew strong deterministic versions. Otherwise, the person would not have a strong case for cognitive freedom.[13] This would not necessitate technological enslavement. However, it should be noted that many who advocate technological oversight also accept a version of materialism that is thoroughly atheistic at heart.[14]

Philosophical Defense for Cognitive Freedom

Philosophically, we have at least three reasons to defend cognitive freedom. The first comes from Thomas Aquinas, who argued for cognitive liberty due to the nature of laws. Aquinas believed in libertarian freedom to some extent—but maybe not to the level of some. By presenting Aquinas's take on the concept, we can show how cognitive liberty fits within a paradigm where God is seen as the First Agent, without deposing God's involvement in the world.

For Aquinas, human freedom of the will is evident. Laws and regulations make little sense if no one is capable of consciously keeping them. Aquinas acknowledges, "Man has free-will: otherwise counsels, exhortations, commands, prohibitions, rewards and punishments would be in vain."[15] According to Aquinas, this freedom does not imply complete independence because he holds to primary and secondary movers. God is the Primary Mover as he is the only Being who exists as pure act (i.e., pure being).[16] As a pure actual Being, everything must initially come from God. Catholic theologian Charles Albert Dubray explains the concept as follows:

> In all finite beings we find actuality and potentiality, perfection and imperfection. Primary matter, which is the basis of material substance, is a pure potentiality. Moreover, change necessarily supposes a potential element, for it is a transition from a state of

13. That is not to say that a defense for cognitive freedom still couldn't be made. However, it would become much more difficult than compatibilist theological paradigms.

14. For instance, certain governments might be more accepting of brain sensors if they have adopted a secularist notion of humanity, seeing people as merely molecules in motion, brains to train rather than human beings. Unfortunately, the cultural shift in worldviews from a Judeo-Christian worldview to a more secular one in the United States leaves Americans more susceptible to similar practices. Theology matters!

15. Aquinas, *Summa Theologica* I.q.83.a1.resp.

16. "There is some first being, whom we call God; and that this first being must be pure act, without the admixture of any potentiality, for the reason that, absolutely, potentiality is posterior to act." Aquinas, *Summa Theologica* I.a9.a1, resp.

> potentiality to a state of actuality; and material things undergo manifold changes in substance, quality, quantity, place, activity, etc. . . . Their existence is contingent. Their actions are successive, and are distinct from a faculty of acting. The fact that all things have in themselves some potentiality warrants the conclusion that there must exist a being, God, from whom potentiality is wholly excluded, and who, therefore, is simply actuality and perfection, *Actus Purus.*[17]

However, people and the natural world have freedom of the will as it pertains to being secondary agents. Aquinas adds, "God works sufficiently in things as a First Agent, but it does not follow from this that the operation of secondary agents is superfluous (or unnecessary)."[18] Working from a Thomistic underpinning, Molina later asserts that God has middle knowledge, the idea that God knows fully what secondary agents would choose to do in certain circumstances.[19] Regardless of how one resolves the issue of God's involvement with human freedom, there is no viable reason to conclude that God's sovereignty removes the cognitive liberty of the human will. Therefore, cognitive freedom is both a biblically and philosophically sound concept.

The second philosophical defense for cognitive liberty comes from the dualist nature of humanity. Those who are materialists operate under the assumption that human life is monistic, meaning that all that exists is the physical body. Monists reject the idea of an immaterial I (i.e., the soul or the self).

While most secular philosophers are monistic, a dualistic renaissance is underway. Dualists hold that life consists of both the material body and the immaterial soul. Herein is the great conundrum. If human beings are monistic, then free will is merely an illusion. Oddly, this is a concept defended by monadic psychologists.[20] But this begs the question: Are those who are alcoholics and drug addicts doomed to their addictions? If so, why do we encourage people to do better? From a counseling perspective, it makes no sense. In contrast, many philosophers acknowledge that there are increasingly good reasons to believe in the immaterial self.

17. Dubray, "Catholic Encyclopedia."

18. Aquinas, *Summa Theologica* I.q105.a5.ad1.

19. For more information on middle knowledge, see Keathley, *Salvation and Sovereignty*, and Craig, *Only Wise God*, 136–37.

20. Psychologist Francis Merson makes the argument that all decisions are determined by past events rather than from cognitive freedom. Merson, "Recognize Free Will Is Illusion."

One such reason is found in the concept of knowledge by acquaintance. Brandon Rickabaugh and J. P. Moreland define knowledge by acquaintance as an awareness of reality. They note, "If I am acquainted with something, then I am directly aware of it; *epistemically direct*—my awareness does not rely on an awareness of anything else, and *metaphysically direct*—my awareness is not mediated by or through anything."[21] This awareness precludes the existence of the immaterial self. Oddly, atheist Bertrand Russell first argued for knowledge by acquaintance.[22] At least fifty-five contemporary philosophers have accepted and defended a substantive theory of acquaintance.[23] While some may lay claim that the theory implicates a monadic take on humanity, such is far from the case. Rickabaugh and Moreland contend that our awareness of external things and internal states of being lays a good claim for substance dualism. They state the following:

> Suppose we have a direct awareness of ourselves as simple, immaterial substances. In that case, we have (i) a strong defense of [substance dualism], (ii) a plausible and explanatory powerful account of why we have the dualist seeming by unifying them around direct awareness of the self, rather than leaving them as a disparate set of isolated intuitions, and (iii) a good explanation for why dualism is the commonsense view, namely, it expresses what people the world over know to be true based on their direct awareness of themselves.[24]

The third philosophical defense for cognitive freedom comes from the enduring nature of the I. Another fascinating argument for the immaterial soul—and thus, cognitive liberty—is the mereological argument for the enduring nature of the soul. Yes, that's a mouthful! Nonetheless, here is the argument in deductive form:

1. If something is a physical object composed of separable parts (an MA), it does not endure over time as the same object if it comes to have different parts.
2. My (a human person's) body and brain are physical objects composed of separate parts.

21. Rickabaugh and Moreland, *Substance of Consciousness*, 94.

22. Rickabaugh and Moreland, *Substance of Consciousness*, 94.

23. Duncan, "Acquaintance," 9.

24. Rickabaugh and Moreland, *Substance of Consciousness*, 116. A fuller defense of substance dualism from self-awareness is given in chapter 5 of their work.

3. Therefore, my body and brain do not endure over time as the same object if they come to have different separable parts.
4. I (a human person) do endure over time as the same object.
5. Therefore, I am not my body or brain.
6. I am either a simple enduring soul or a body or a brain.
7. Therefore, I am a simple enduring soul.[25]

Let's explain. The argument begins with the premise that a physical object is composed of different parts that eventually change over time. Our bodies are remarkable machines. The skin cells regenerate every seven to ten years, whereas the cells in our skeletal muscles regenerate every fifteen years.[26] Simply speaking, if you're over fifteen years of age, your body is not the same as it was fifteen years ago. Thus, premises 1–3 hold.

So, this leads us to premise 5. Are we the same people that we were fifteen years ago? Granted, our experiences mold us. Nonetheless, the conscious self, or the I, remains the same. I am writing this chapter in 2024. Fifteen years ago, I lived in a different house, in a different place, held far fewer degrees (not even holding a bachelor's degree at that time), and was working a different job. In some ways, life was a bit simpler back then, but I digress. Then, my body was much stronger than it is now and without nearly as many health problems. Despite all those differences, I am still the same person (Brian Chilton) that I was in 2009.

Let's look at this in a different light. Suppose I had committed a crime back in 2009 (which I didn't). And let's say that I was never convicted of that crime until 2024. Even though fifteen years had elapsed since the crime had occurred, could I be held accountable for that crime given a materialistic monism? Since the body completely changes every fifteen years, a defense attorney could claim that since my body changed, then I am not the same person and, therefore, I could not be held responsible for the actions of my former self. I doubt there is a jury out there that would buy that argument. However, that is exactly what materialistic monism claims. Thus, as human beings, our true selves endure over time (premise 4), indicating that we are more than our bodies and brains (premise 5). Since we must either be our bodies or enduring souls (premise 6) and given that materialism does not hold in this case, then we must be enduring, immaterial souls (premise 7).

25. Rickabaugh and Moreland, *Substance of Consciousness*, 145–46.

26. Quest Diagnostics, "Do My Cells Really Change."

The enduring nature of the soul leads to a form of libertarian freedom that Rickabaugh and Moreland call staunch libertarian agency (SLA).[27] They offer the following as an argument for SLA, aptly named the SLA Argument.

1. If human persons are wholly physical objects (e.g., a brain or a body), then they do not have SLA.
2. But human persons do have SLA.
3. Therefore, human persons are not wholly physical objects.
4. Human persons either are wholly physical objects, or they are (or have) simple enduring souls.
5. Therefore, human persons are (or have) simple enduring souls.[28]

As we previously noted, human beings have some form of freedom of the will, even if understood from a compatibilist backdrop (premise 2). Premise 1 is commonsensical and need not be defended. Premises 3 and 4 are warranted given premise 2. Thus, conclusion 5 stands to reason. As such, people do have some form of freedom of the will that should be preserved and defended as it is a hallmark of their soulish, immaterial self.

Why does this matter? As A. C. Ewing suggests, only an enduring I (i.e., the soul) can account for the conscious self; that is, "there must be a single being persisting through the process to grasp a proposition or inference as a whole."[29] In other words, Rickabaugh and Moreland state, "Intellectual responsibility seems to presuppose an enduring I."[30] Thus, since human beings have immaterial, conscious souls, then we all have the right and responsibility to maintain our cognitive liberties. No one has the right to interfere with the sacredness of our mental thoughts, the inner workings of the mind, and the freedom each person holds to draw conclusions from the given data. Ironically, brain sensors *could* be found to interfere with the very thing that makes us who we are—enduring, cognitive, conscious beings. Let's dive into this topic a bit more in the next section.

27. Rickabaugh and Moreland, *Substance of Consciousness*, 235.

28. Rickabaugh and Moreland, *Substance of Consciousness*, 237.

29. Ewing, *Value and Reality*, 84.

30. Rickabaugh and Moreland, *Substance of Consciousness*, 162.

COGNITIVE FREEDOM AND WHY IT MATTERS

As noted in the previous section, human beings are individuals endowed with a conscious soul, which entails the ability to freely make decisions, at least within certain parameters. This ability is both philosophically and biblically sound. Additionally, the conscious "I" is commonsensical. Given the criteria listed above, the freedom of one's cognition and mentality are critical as we navigate these complicated waters regarding brain sensors and future technological advancements that could impact these freedoms. These mental freedoms matter for at least five reasons.

The Sacredness of the Mind as a Sanctuary for the Soul

First, the mind is like a sanctuary for the soul. In times of war, it is seen as an unspeakably horrific action if a military entity attacks their enemy in a house of worship. Sanctuaries are often viewed as an untouchable place, as it is held sacred by those who worship there. In a similar manner, the mind is the sanctuary of the soul since it safeguards a person's thoughts and opinions.

I'm sure you have known a person who has been known to have no filter. By this, of course, it is meant that the person in question says what they think without acknowledging how their words may hurt another person. After a while, such a person may find that few people want to associate with him or her, as the person has become a very volatile individual. Well, imagine if every thought you have was broadcast to the world—or at least the one reading the report from your thoughts. Would you want every single thought you hold to be known by everyone?

What about intellectual property? Imagine for a moment that you are using a brain censor. You have an ingenious idea that you would like to promote. However, the person accessing your mental thoughts captures your idea. Now, suppose the thought thief steals your idea and promotes it as their own. Without proper channels in place, there would be no way to accurately identify whose idea it was. It may have been your own. But if you didn't document the idea, you have no way of proving it belonged to you. Here again, the mind is a sanctuary of the soul that should be protected.

The Freedom of Conscious Worship

The second reason complements the first. For this one, we will call it the freedom of conscious worship. This entails two aspects. The first pertains to worship itself. Several passages of Scripture speak on the importance of meditating on the word of God. Joshua acknowledges that Scripture is a book of instruction, and people "are to meditate on it day and night so that you may carefully observe everything written in it. For then you will prosper and succeed in whatever you do" (Josh 1:8). The psalmist also states that the wise person is one who delights in the Lord's instruction and "meditates on it day and night" (Ps 1:2). Another psalmist prays that he will "meditate on [God's] precepts and think about [his] ways" (Ps 119:15). This meditation includes a mental and heartfelt devotion to God through the reading of Scripture, meditating on it, and communicating with God by prayer. Through the mind and spirit, a person communicates with God and hears back from God. Just as a congregant should have the ability to have private conversations with their pastor, likewise, a person's conversations with God should be sacred and holy. No one should be able to hinder or disrupt a person's deeply personal relationship with God. For this reason, society and researchers should exercise great caution before giving away the mental freedoms we hold as people.

A second component of conscious worship includes personal convictions. By this, I mean that a person has the rights and freedoms to worship as they choose and to maintain their own interpretations and convictions about God and the world. I have taught several lessons on offering spiritual and cultural assessments in a clinical setting. One of the main emphases of these assessments is that when observing a person's spiritual and cultural background, the clinician must never assume that one knows the beliefs and rituals cherished by the individual in question. Never assume.

For instance, I attended a church years ago in the mountains of North Carolina. The pastor delivered a biblical message that was, to a degree, intermingled with conservative political underpinnings. I cannot say that the pastor was shy about the political innuendos of his message, as he hammered down on some controversial topics. Most of the church praised the pastor with a chorus of "Amens."

After the service had concluded, we ate at a local restaurant to celebrate the birthday of a beloved family member. As we were waiting for our meal, I overheard the conversation of two individuals who had attended the service that morning. I quickly became aware that one of the congregants was beside herself, fuming with anger. She did not appreciate the pastor's comments and thought they were inappropriate for the service. Given that most of the church had previously sung the pastor's praises, one would not realize that some congregants were angry while sitting in the sanctuary that day.

Another example is pertinent to our case. At a facility, I was recently approached with the possibility of officiating the wedding for a local couple. However, I was concerned that if I officiated this ceremony that I would be required to officiate all ceremonies that came through the facility. Being that I am a conservative Christian, I have parameters around what kind of wedding ceremonies I officiate. Given that I normally do not discuss political conversations[31] and that I have delivered lessons on how to minister to all kinds of people, some had assumed that I would likely officiate any kind of wedding ceremony. Far from the case!

Whether the pastor was right or wrong in his judgment or whether I am right in my marital convictions is beside the point. The primary matter at hand is that each person has the mental freedom to maintain their own given personal convictions, to form their own conclusions, and to worship in the manner of their choosing. It was upon this very freedom of conscience that our nation was built.

One may ask, "Don't Americans believe the same kind of things about God?" Such is far from the case. Two Baylor sociologists recently reviewed a survey that showed that Americans differ in their conceptions of God. To illustrate how different Americans view God, they offered an illustration of how two women, named Theresa and Trudy, view the judgment of God.

According to Theresa, a middle-aged African American who lives in a working-class neighborhood,[32] God is vengeful, judgmental, and stands opposed to any wrongdoing. She goes on to say, "God doesn't like it when people sin, and if they keep doing the same sins over and over, he will punish them to let them know they are sinning."[33]

31. The reason that I do not talk much about politics to the general populace is that I have found that most people are not emotionally strong enough to carry on intelligent conversations with whom they disagree. These conversations can quickly escalate to emotional outbursts, hurt feelings, and damaged relationships. I typically observe how a person interacts with others, especially in disagreements. If a person handles oneself well, then I might enter the political foray. Otherwise, I keep my thoughts to myself. Which, quite frankly, is another reason why we should not give away our mental cognitive freedoms.

32. Froese and Bader, *America's Four Gods*, 18.

33. Froese and Bader, *America's Four Gods*, 18.

However, according to Trudy, a lifelong Methodist and suburban mother of three, God is far more loving and kind. Trudy maintains, "My vision is not of a God filled with anger or hatred. I don't know that I would say God feels disappointment, but I believe God wants the best for everyone and tries to make that happen."[34] Along with Trudy, a woman named Sarah, an active church member from Rhode Island, asserts, "I don't believe that God is an angry, wrathful God. That's just been a construct of people. . . . As far as zapping people with lightning bolts, I don't believe that that happens."[35]

From the observations of Froese and Bader, Americans view God in four different ways: an Authoritarian God, a Benevolent God, a Critical God, and a Distant God.[36] Thirty-one percent of Americans believe in an Authoritarian God,[37] a God who is active in the world and judgmental. Typically, extreme fundamentalists fit within this category. They will assert that sin brings about instant divine judgment into the world.

Twenty-four percent of Americans uphold a view of a Benevolent God.[38] In this view, God is active in the world and is loving and kind. The Benevolent God actively pursues the good for all people. Evangelicals largely constitute membership of this category. While those in this section may still believe in some form of judgment, they hold that love is the driving factor behind what God does.

Sixteen percent of Americans accept the existence of a Critical God.[39] A Critical God is one who is slow to bring judgment, but eventually will. Froese and Bader consider the 2007 address of Pope Benedict XVI and those of Pope John Paul II to uphold the critical view of God. Seeing that injustices still occur, those of this mindset await a time when God will set all things right.

Twenty-four percent of Americans maintain the belief in a Distant God.[40] The Distant conception of God fits within the parameters of Deism, Eastern mysticism, New Age thought, and even those who are otherwise agnostic may find themselves within this category. Theologian Paul Tillich

34. Froese and Bader, *America's Four Gods*, 19.

35. Froese and Bader, *America's Four Gods*, 18–19.

36. Froese and Bader, *America's Four Gods*, 26.

37. The statistics in this section came from BRS, as reported by Berger, "America's Four Gods."

38. Froese and Bader, *America's Four Gods*, 29.

39. Froese and Bader, *America's Four Gods*, 31.

40. Froese and Bader, *America's Four Gods*, 33.

would also fit within this category.[41] Believers in the Distant God may see God as more of a personal force or an unknowable transcendence that cannot be fully known by humanity. As such, God is concerned with all creation, but God does not intervene in the affairs of humankind and certainly does not require praise and worship. An additional 5 percent consider themselves strict atheists.[42]

The reason this study is important is that it reveals how different Americans view God. Within your own congregation, it is highly likely that you will have members who hold either the Authoritarian, Benevolent, Critical, or Distant view of God, and perhaps a smorgasbord of all four. Even still, each person should have certain freedoms of worship as it pertains to each person's mental cognitive abilities. Walter Shurden laid out four fragile freedoms set in place as it pertains to worship, which seems very relevant here:

> BIBLE FREEDOM is the historic Baptist affirmation that the Bible, under the Lordship of Christ, must be central in the life of the individual and church and that Christians, with the best and most scholarly tools of inquiry, are both free and obligated to study and obey the Scripture.
>
> SOUL FREEDOM is the historic affirmation of the inalienable right and responsibility of every person to deal with God without the imposition of creed, the interference of clergy, or the intervention of civil government.
>
> CHURCH FREEDOM is the historic Baptist affirmation that local churches are free, under the Lordship of Christ, to determine their membership and leadership, to order their worship and work. . . .
>
> RELIGIOUS FREEDOM is the historic Baptist affirmation of freedom OF religion, freedom FOR religion, and freedom FROM religion, insisting that Caesar is not Christ and Christ is not Caesar.[43]

While we may differ on certain aspects of these four freedoms as they pertain to the implementation of creeds to safeguard religious doctrine, even then, a person is free to subject oneself to the creed in question. America

41. Froese and Bader, *America's Four Gods*, 34.

42. Froese and Bader, *America's Four Gods*, 34.

43. Shurden, *Baptist Identity*, 5. Capitalization in original.

was built upon the understanding that each person holds unalienable rights regarding religion. If we, as a society, allow technology to have too much control in our mental cognitive freedoms, who is to say that a government, church, or corporation could not monitor our most sacred beliefs in an attempt to conform us in their image rather than God's?

Before you say that could not happen, remember the control that the Catholic church held over Europeans in the Holy Roman Empire. Also, consider the strong control that the Church of England lorded over the ecclesial lives of early American colonies. If you think that this could not happen, simply look back at our history. You will find abundant cases of authoritarian figures attempting to exercise full control over the citizens of various lands. Is this something we are willing to give away? Just as a reminder, these freedoms are more easily given away than they are to reclaim.

The Freedom to Disengage: Medical Interactions with Health and Behavior

Third, our cognitive freedoms do not just apply to our inner world of mentality. It also applies to our overall health. Consider the latest medical research that I obtained from a good friend who serves as a nurse practitioner. She shared the following report with me that comes from the *Pediatrics* medical journal. It speaks of the importance of removing technological devices from a child's room to allow for better sleep and rest.

> Bedtime routines—Establishment of a consistent bedtime routine is helpful for all manifestations of behavioral insomnia (bedtime resistance, prolonged sleep onset, and night wakings). The routine should last approximately 20 to 45 minutes and include three to four soothing activities, such as taking a bath, changing into pajamas, and reading stories; it should not include television or other electronic devices. The introduction at bedtime of more appropriate sleep associations should be readily available to the child during the night and can include transitional objects such as a blanket or toy. The child should be put to bed drowsy but awake to minimize dependence upon parental presence at sleep onset.
>
> An integral part of the bedtime routine is the institution of a bedtime and sleep schedule that ensures a developmentally appropriate amount of sleep. The bedtime should coincide with the child's natural sleep onset time. A consistent nightly bedtime will help

> to reinforce the circadian clock and enable the child to fall asleep more easily.[44]

Another important study found that children needed to abstain from technology at least ninety minutes before sleep:

> Screen time accounted for one third of the 90 minutes before sleep onset in New Zealand young people aged 5 to 18 years. Higher engagement was evident in participants with a later sleep onset, suggesting that reducing screen sedentary time may be an appropriate intervention for promoting earlier sleep onset in young people.[45]

Now suppose that a child had a technological device implanted in their body. They would not be able to escape the temptation of the technology in question. In fact—if taken too far—the child would never have the ability to disengage from technology.

Personally, I have found that taking technology fasts to be beneficial. A technology fast is a specific time spent away from phones, computers, and tablets. This time is generally spent in nature, most often around a fire pit or taking a hike in the woods. A person often feels rejuvenated after having been "unplugged" from the outside world. I have also observed that children are more agitated if they have too much screen time, as opposed to spending time outdoors. The same is true for adults, too.

Certainly, there is a mind-body connection. If we do not care for our mental and cognitive health, especially by taking breaks from our devices, then we could suffer physical health problems. In fact, we already are. I do not have to remind you of the mental health crisis that we have in our nation right now. According to the National Alliance on Mental Illness, 22.8 percent of adults in the United States suffered from some mental illness in 2021.[46] This accounts for 57.8 million people and represents one in five adults. Studies suggest that prolonged technology use can lead to various mental health issues, such as anxiety, depression, and social isolation, among other things.[47] If this is true with technological devices remaining separate from our biology, it begs to ask, how much more would the integration of technology and biology negatively affect the mental health of Americans

44. Mindell and Owens, "Clinical Guide to Pediatric Sleep," 332–33.
45. Foley et al., "Presleep activities," 281.
46. NAMI, "Mental Health by the Numbers."
47. Kinghorn, "Impact of Heavy Technology Use."

and those who participate worldwide? Could it be that the negative impacts outweigh any potential benefit? It's something worth considering.

Further Degradation of Work-Life Balance by Businesses and Organizations

Fourth, we also need to consider the impact that brain sensors could have on the work-life balance of employees if their corporations implement these devices into the modern workforce. Studies consistently show that Americans, on average, work far more hours than their European counterparts. In a report from the International Labour Organization (ILO)—a United Nations agency—Americans worked around 1,750 hours per year, compared to Germans who worked about 1,350 hours per year.[48] If monitors are implanted in a person's body, then how could a person ever maintain a true work-life balance?

It could be argued that removable sensors may not be as intrusive. While that's true, would even temporary sensors allow an organization access to the inner workings of a person's mind? Consider the impact that social media has had on the modern workforce. Employees have been fired from their jobs because of public posts they shared on Facebook and other social media outlets. For instance, British teen Kimberley Swann learned the importance of filtering her posts on social media. On her first day of work, Swann could not help but post on Facebook about how boring she found her new job. Unfortunately for Swann, her employer, Mr. Ivell, read her post while surfing the internet and promptly fired her afterward.[49] Multiple other stories could be shared. Nonetheless, this leads to a question that must be considered: Could employers fire employees for their thoughts and mentality if brain sensors are used? Furthermore, are people not entitled to form their own opinions without the oversight of their supervisors? While I do not necessarily have the answers to these questions, they are concepts that must be considered before organizations and institutions begin tinkering with the idea of brain sensors. And organizations must consider the backlash that could, and likely *should*, come from the use of these devices. Lest we forget, numerous healthcare agencies faced an exodus of employees once it was mandated that employees should take the COVID-19 vaccine. One would think that it would be highly likely that an even greater exodus

48. Grieve, "Americans Work Hundreds of Hours."

49. Reid, "People Who Got Fired."

would come if organizations began talking about the use of brain sensors and, especially, implants.[50] Additionally, we should also consider the laws that had to be developed during the Industrial Revolution to keep young children from being overworked in the factories, and to provide good working conditions for employees across the nation. In this writer's opinion, cognitive liberty fits well within the realm of the very same parameters. Mental enslavement is what we're talking about.

The Rise of Technarchy

Cultural critic Neil Postman is often known for his book *Amusing Ourselves to Death*, and rightfully so; it's an amazing work. However, Postman also wrote an equally compelling book entitled *Technopoly: The Surrender of Culture to Technology*. In *Technopoly*, Postman contends that human civilization has often held an unhealthy relationship with its technology. He maintains that civilization can be broken into three forms of society. The first category is tool-using cultures, where people use their devices to assist with everyday life and/or survival.[51] However, humanity's dependence on technology grew to the point that technology became a dominant and integral part of society. Postman calls this second category "technocracy." According to Postman, this age began with Francis Bacon in 1561.[52] Bacon was arguably one of the first to promote the idea that technology could improve human happiness.[53] Eventually, mankind's dependence on technology grew to the point that a third category was introduced, one he calls "technopoly."[54] Technopoly is defined as a "state of culture. It is also a state of mind. It consists in the deification of technology, which means that the culture seeks its authorization in technology, finds its satisfactions in technology, and takes its orders from technology."[55] Postman goes on to say, "This requires the development of a new kind of social order, and of necessity leads to the rapid dissolution of much that is associated with

50. Quite frankly, I would likely be one of those who would join such an exodus given the complexities of this issue.

51. Postman, *Technopoly*, 25.

52. Postman, *Technopoly*, 35.

53. Postman, *Technopoly*, 35.

54. Postman, *Technopoly*, 20.

55. Postman, *Technopoly*, 71.

traditional beliefs."[56] Therefore, technological advancements become the most important measure of human achievement.[57]

Given Postman's three-tiered view of cultural dependence on technology, I think we can deduce that something has happened over the past few years that has introduced a fourth category to Postman's three-tiered hierarchy. I argue that we are on the cusp of what could be called *technarcy*[58] or *techtatorship*.[59] Technarchy describes a society that has given technology a place of leadership over the human race, even to the point that commonplace ideals, traditions, and mores are replaced to allow the full integration of technology and biology. Technarchy could lend itself to a techtatorship, a more oppressive form of life, where technology exercises supreme control over humanity. Mind you, technology and technological devices are not the problem. Our use of technology is.

If society degenerates to a technarchy, we could expect even more overarching "big brother" programs where the government intrudes into a person's life in his most sacred form—the thoughts and ideas of its civilians. Not to be an alarmist but simply serving as the voice of a historian (my doctoral minor was in the field of history), we have several examples in history where governmental agencies try to micromanage the lives of each citizen. In Nazi Germany, Hitler and his goons expected everyone to adopt the Nazi philosophy. Adversaries could find themselves imprisoned or killed. Dietrich Bonhoeffer is one such example. In modern dictatorships, religious beliefs are controlled and monitored by those in authority. But what happens when the government has access to each person's movements and, if possible, the inner sanctum of a person's mind? In modern America, we have already seen what happens if a person opposes the trends spewed forth by political correctness advocates. A person can be sued, fined, or canceled. In one fell swoop, an individual can lose almost everything they've worked for just by simply holding an opposing opinion. Do we really want to allow governments, corporations, and institutions that kind of access to our mental freedoms? Keep in mind, there is no turning back once Pandora's box is opened.

56. Postman, *Technopoly*, 71.

57. Postman, *Technopoly*, 71.

58. Technarchy combines the words "technology" and "anarchy."

59. Technarchy seems to flow off the tongue a bit better, so we will use that term rather than its counterpart.

A BIBLICAL CALL TO FREEDOM

Before wrapping up, we should take a moment to reiterate the biblical emphasis placed on freedom. Earlier, we spoke on the importance of our cognitive freedoms from a biblical perspective. But what about freedom in general?

Throughout the pages of Scripture, God is often seen working to bring freedom to people. Consider the story of the exodus. Yahweh delivered his people from Egyptian enslavement. Even through parting the waves of the Red Sea, God went to extraordinary means to bring freedom to the Hebrews. The people were freed, and the story of the exodus continued to impact the culture of the Israelites for generations.

Consistently, the people were told to remember what God had done for them to bring them out of bondage. Moses instructed the people to "remember this day when you came out of Egypt, out of the place of slavery, for the Lord brought you out of here by the strength of his hand" (Exod 13:3). Their remembrance of this event was so imperative that the fourth commandment included an admonition to "remember that you were a slave in the land of Egypt, and the Lord your God brought you out of there with a strong hand and an outstretched arm. That is what the Lord your God has commanded you to keep the Sabbath day" (Deut 5:15).[60]

Another great example is found in the work and ministry of Jesus. Jesus stood against oppression and stood up for those that the government and religion of the day had forsaken. In John 4, Jesus ministered to a Samaritan woman at Jacob's well. The unnamed woman was startled, even asking, "How is it that you, a Jew, ask for a drink from me, a Samaritan woman? . . . For Jews do not associate with Samaritans" (John 4:9). Jesus later revealed himself to be the Messiah, leading to the woman's conversion. When the woman experienced the freedom that God brought to her, she went into the community that had abandoned her and spread the gospel. Because of her testimony, the "town believed in him . . . when she testified, 'He told me everything I ever did'" (John 4:39). Jesus overturned the money tables in the temple because he viewed the practice of the religious leaders to be oppressive. For Jesus, God's temple was supposed to be a "house of prayer," but they had turned it into a "den of thieves" (Matt 21:13). Additionally, Jesus taught that people who believe in him will "know the truth, and the truth will set you free" (John 8:32).

60. Other examples include Josh 24:17 and Ps 105:38.

Other biblical passages stress the importance of freedom. Paul stated, "For freedom, Christ set us free. Stand firm, then, and don't submit again to a yoke of slavery" (Gal 5:1). In this text, Paul speaks against the Judaizers of his day who attempted to lead people back into legalism instead of the grace of God. In another epistle, Paul notes that "the Lord is the Spirit, and where the Spirit of the Lord is, there is freedom" (2 Cor 3:17). Because of the freedom found in Christ, "there is now no condemnation for those in Christ Jesus, because the law of the Spirit of life in Christ Jesus has set you free from the law of sin and death" (Rom 8:1–2). I could go on and on.

This little excursus is merely to show the importance of freedom found in our relationship with God. It also shows the freedom that God affords. Since part of this freedom includes the freedom of the Spirit and of our mental cognitive abilities preserved and freed by the Spirit of God, then we must ask if, by succumbing ourselves completely to any form of technology that could interfere with our spiritual and/or cognitive abilities, are we, thereby, enslaving ourselves to something that could impede with these divinely given freedoms? As with the Galatians near brush with legalistic enslavement at the hands of the Judaizers of their day, are we, too, in danger of placing a yoke upon ourselves from which Christ freed us? It's something to consider.

CONCLUSION

As we consider brain sensors and their impact, a humorous scene from the movie *Dinner with Schmucks* comes to mind. Parents beware, the movie is not for young children. Some of the movie's humor is a bit crude. The movie centers around Tim (played by Paul Rudd), an aspiring business executive who is pursuing a promotion to the "big leagues" of his organization. However, to do so, he must participate in a bizarre practice in which executives choose individuals whom they perceive to be idiots (or schmucks) to entertain them over dinner with their insane gifts. At the end of the night, the CEO of the organization, Lance Fender (played by Bruce Greenwood), crowns the most special person—or schmuck—of the evening. Even though Tim's girlfriend, Julie (played by Stephanie Szostak), tells him not to participate in the dinner, due to the offensive nature of the activity, Tim's aspirations to succeed get the best of him, especially after he meets a particularly intriguing person named Barry (played by Steve Carell).

Barry's "gift" was to tell stories through dead mice that he embalmed and positioned into different scenes.

During the dinner, Barry succumbed to the so-called mind control tactics of his bully-ish coworker named Therman (played by North Carolina native Zach Galifianakis). Therman convinced Barry that he was able to control him using his mental prowess. It was not until later that Tim convinced Barry that he had something better than mind control; he had brain control. Tim suggested that Barry could lay "brain worms" into a person's mind. Tim's pep talk encouraged Barry to stand up against his bully, leading to the hilarious hijinks of Barry shooting invisible brain control beams toward Therman, and Therman doing the same with his invisible mind control efforts. Lance then crowned Barry as the evening's most extraordinary person.[61]

Writing this chapter almost feels like we are caught between the war of Therman's "mind control" vs. Barry's "brain control." It seems so bizarre to think that we have reached a point in human civilization where such things as brain sensors are even possible. But we have. And we are.

As noted in this chapter, we have biblical and philosophical reasons to believe that we as human beings maintain at least some degree of cognitive freedom. From a biblical perspective, God has worked in numerous ways to offer spiritual freedom to the world through Christ. However, brain censors have the potential to hinder these freedoms, especially if misused.

This book has emphasized throughout its pages that technology is not necessarily bad. The same is true for implants and brain sensors. When used appropriately, brain sensors can offer those who suffer various physical maladies an opportunity to communicate and lead a somewhat normal life. Let the reader understand that I am in no way opposed to technology that may benefit the health and vitality of humanity. However, as with all things, the problem is not with the instrument, but, rather, the issue arises with how any form of instrumentation is used. Just as one cannot blame a gun for the shooting of an innocent person, likewise, we cannot blame technology for humanity's misuse of it.

Nonetheless, those of us who are a bit cynical and leery of these advances are always needed. Why? Well, Postman says it best. When speaking of a technopolic society, he says, "As the power of traditional social institutions to organize perceptions and judgment declines, bureaucracies, expertise, and technical machinery become the principal means by which

61. Roach, *Dinner for Schmucks.*

Technopoly hopes to control information and thereby provide itself with intelligibility and order."[62] Postman's words were penned in 1992, some thirty-two years before this book was published. As previously noted, if we are not careful, a technopoly society can become a technarcy, where our ideas, thoughts, and beliefs are controlled by those who manage the technological devices we use. If we are talking about installing devices into our bodies and brains, then we are opening Pandora's box to a type of enslavement to a degree that the world has never seen. As a theologian and historian, my concern is not with the technology. Instead, my fear is with those who manage the technology. For further insights into how humans have abused technology and used it against others, only open a history book. It won't take you long to find numerous examples. And that, my friends, is the basis of my concern.

BIBLIOGRAPHY

Aquinas, Thomas. *Summa Theologica*. Translated by the Fathers of the English Dominican Province. London: Burns Oates & Washbourne, 1920.

Berger, Ron. "America's Four Gods." Wise Guys, Dec. 27, 2016. https://web.archive.org/web/20161228072225/https://wiseguys2015.com/2016/12/27/americas-four-gods/.

Craig, William Lane. *The Only Wise God: The Compatibility of Divine Foreknowledge and Human Freedom*. Eugene, OR: Wipf & Stock, 2000.

Dubray, Charles Albert. "Catholic Encyclopedia (1913)/ Actus Purus." Wikisource. https://en.wikisource.org/wiki/Catholic_Encyclopedia_(1913)/Actus_Purus.

Duncan, Matt. "Acquaintance." *Philosophy Compass* 16 (2021) e12727. https://doi.org/10.1111/phc3.12727.

Ewing, A. C. *Value and Reality*. London: George Allen and Unwin, 1973.

Foley, L. S., et al. "Presleep Activities and Time of Sleep Onset in Children." *Pediatrics* 131.2 (2013) 276–82.

Froese, Paul, and Christopher Bader. *America's Four Gods: What We Say About God—and What That Says About Us*. Oxford: Oxford University Press, 2010.

Golgowski, Nina. "Neuralink Reveals Issues with First Human Brain Implant After Surgery." HuffPost, May 10, 2024. https://www.huffpost.com/entry/neuralink-implant-had-issues-after-first-human-surgery_n_663d23c1e4b0c38baf0f7716.

Grieve, Pete. "Americans Work Hundreds of Hours More a Year than Europeans: Report." Money, Jan. 6, 2023. https://money.com/americans-work-hours-vs-europe-china/.

Keathley, Kenneth D. *Salvation and Sovereignty: A Molinist Approach*. Nashville: B&H Academic, 2010.

Kinghorn, Kathy. "The Impact of Heavy Technology Use on Mental Health: Understanding the Risks." Therapy Utah, June 27, 2023. https://therapyutah.org/impact-of-heavy-technology-use-on-mental-health/.

62. Postman, *Technopoly*, 90–91.

Merson, Francis. "Recognise Free Will Is an Illusion and Reap the Emotional Benefits." Psyche, Oct. 12, 2023. https://psyche.co/ideas/recognise-free-will-is-an-illusion-and-reap-the-emotional-benefits.

National Alliance on Mental Health (NAMI). "Mental Health by the Numbers." https://www.nami.org/about-mental-illness/mental-health-by-the-numbers/.

Peters, Gretchen. "Independence Day." Track 4 on Martina McBride, *The Way That I Am*, RCA Nashville, 1994. lyrics.com/lyric/35347478/Martina+McBride/Independence+Day.

Postman, Neil. *Amusing Ourselves to Death: Public Discourse in an Age of Show Business.* New York: Penguin, 1986.

———. *Technopoly: The Surrender of Culture to Technology.* New York: Vintage, 1992.

Quest Diagnostics. "Do My Cells Really Change Every 7 Years?" Feb. 21, 2023. https://www.questdiagnostics.com/patients/blog/articles/do-my-cells-really-change-every-7-years.

Reid, L. M. "Stories of People Who Got Fired for Their Facebook Comments." HubPages, May 27, 2024.

Rickabaugh, Brandon, and J. P. Moreland. *The Substance of Consciousness: A Comprehensive Defense of Contemporary Substance Dualism.* Hoboken, NJ: Wiley-Blackwell, 2024.

Roach, Jay, dir. *Dinner for Schmucks.* Hollywood: Paramount, 2010.

Shurden, Walter B. *The Baptist Identity: Four Fragile Freedoms.* Macon, GA: Smyth & Helwys, 2013.

Sriram, Akash, and Kaniyik Ghosh. "Elon Musk's Neuralink Implants Brain Chip in First Human." Reuters, Jan. 30, 2024. https://www.reuters.com/technology/neuralink-implants-brain-chip-first-human-musk-says-2024-01-29/.

Stuart, Douglas K. *Exodus.* Vol. 2. The New American Commentary. Nashville: B&H, 2006.

Terry, Mark. "BrainGate's Technology Allows Quadriplegic Individuals to Control a Tablet With Their Thoughts." BioSpace, Nov. 26, 2018. https://www.biospace.com/article/braingate-successfully-tested-a-brain-computer-interface-for-quadriplegics/.

Wexler, Bruce E. "Mind Control in China's Classrooms." Yale Global, Dec. 3, 2019. https://archive-yaleglobal.yale.edu/content/mind-control-chinas-classrooms.

5

Stewarding the Merging of Technology with Humanity

Deanna Huff, PhD

There are two basic loves: love of God to forgetfulness of self *or* love of self to forgetfulness of God.

—St. Augustine

People have sought human enhancement for decades. The word "enhancement" used to mean anything from supplements to anti-aging products designed to improve the body; that definition has since changed. It is natural for people to care about their physical health. People often strive to achieve good health by eating a well-balanced diet and engaging in physical exercise. Today, many people wear AI devices to monitor physical activities, regulate sleep patterns, and achieve their health goals. AI wearable devices can fall under the category of biotechnology, which is the external integration of devices with the body. It is not wrong to care about one's health, but some people desire to advance humanity into a new era, striving to merge technology with humans to make them stronger, faster, and live longer. These advancements are often referred to as *enhancements*, but this term has taken on a new meaning in our modern world with AI. For the purpose of this chapter, we will define human *enhancement* as "biomedical (relating to biology and medicine) interventions that are used to improve human form or functioning beyond what is necessary to restore or sustain health."[1] Let us not confuse healing or *repairing* the body with modern-day human *enhancement*. By human *enhancement*, we are referring to pushing the body beyond its inherent capabilities. As Christians who value life, we surely want to cure sickness and save lives. We want to use advanced technology to mitigate pain and suffering, but the goal is for healthy living rather than superior and eternal beings. The idea that humans can attain superhuman capabilities is not new. In the garden of Eden, Adam and Eve incorrectly thought that if they followed the serpent's instructions, they could "become like gods" (Gen 3:5).[2] Since the garden of Eden, Satan has tempted mankind to dethrone God and enthrone man. He tempts humanity to have disordered loves.[3] His desire is for people to trust in technology and themselves for a better life rather than in God. Now, the temptation is before us to either recognize what it means to be human through the lens of the Bible or seek to develop a god-man through the merging of technology and humanity. The questions lie before us: What temptations are before us? What does it mean to be human? Did God give our bodies limitations for a good reason and for his glory? How can we attain eternal life? Does the Bible speak to the new technology available to us today?

Human *enhancements* can include wearable health devices, cosmetic surgery, performance-enhancing drugs, gene editing, and other technologies. But there is a group known as transhumanists that aims not only for "healthy longevity, but they are also striving for unlimited lifespans for all humanity."[4] Could it be that the method of *enhancements* and the transhumanism movement is the devil's bargaining chip for life eternal?[5] Is Satan asking if we will only give our bodies over to him to make them healthier, stronger, and faster, then we can receive the promise of happiness and eternal life? Is he tempting humanity once again, offering something that

1. Juengst and Moseley, "Human Enhancement," para. 4.

2. Unless otherwise noted, Scripture quoted in this chapter is from the New American Standard Bible (NASB).

3. The idea of Disordered Loves and Reordered Loves first originated from the book by Naugle, *Reordered Love, Reordered Lives*. I have used the book's theme to expand this chapter.

4. Humanity Plus, "Our Mission."

5. Waters, *This Mortal Flesh*, 101.

could be destructive to humanity? We need to proceed with caution when considering the subjects of utilizing *enhancement* methods, but we need to reject the ideology of transhumanism. If we turn to the Bible for insight and wisdom, then we see that Satan tempts humanity with the idea that we can be the greatest of humans. We can be like gods, and we can rule the world (more on these two temptations further in the chapter). Some transhumanists believe being human should not be the endpoint of humanity and that by merging humans with AI technology, humanity can take the next step in evolution. Nick Bostrom once summarized a core belief of the ideology: "Transhumanists view human nature as a work-in-progress, a half-baked beginning that we can learn to remold in desirable ways. Current humanity need not be the endpoint of evolution."[6] Some transhumanists aim at overcoming death. Yuval Harari claims, "An increasing minority of scientists and thinkers consequently speak more openly these days, and state that the flagship enterprise of modern science is to defeat death and grant humans eternal life."[7] What cost will it be for humans in the process of trying to succeed? This chapter will address the temptations before us through *enhancements* to the body, identify what it means to be human, and explain how God reorders our loves to glorify him in the context of *enhancements*. Human *enhancement* and transhumanist goals may offer something that sounds good, but the Bible provides better guiding principles to help counter the false promises of a better life. Christianity offers the way to a righteous, reordered, and eternal life.

THE TEMPTATIONS

The Inconsolable Longing

Since the beginning of time, humanity has sought to develop technology and improve human life. There is a continuous desire to make the world a better place, as if there is a perfect world that humanity is seeking to attain. Are the desires for human improvement, wellness, and eternal living signposts pointing to the idea that humanity was meant for a healthy and eternal life? A world where suffering no longer exists and youthfulness lasts forever? This desire, this longing in people who seek to enhance their bodies and extend their lives with AI technology, could be a signpost pointing

6. Bostrom, "Transhumanist Values," para. 3.

7. Harari, *Homo Deus*, 27.

us to a transcendent world. Is there a world where forever is a possibility and joy is eternal?

In the book *Surprised by Joy*, C. S. Lewis wrote about inconsolable longings. Longings that people are always seeking to fulfill, but they never seem to attain endless satisfaction. He focused on the idea of joy being an inconsolable longing. He wrote, "All Joy reminds. It is never a possession, always a desire for something longer ago or further away still 'about to be.'"[8] Could it be that the desires of perfect wellness and eternality exist because there is a place in which those desires can be satisfied? Lewis writes, "When a baby feels hunger, well, there is such a thing as food. A duckling wants to swim; well, there is such a thing as water. If I find in myself a desire which no experience in this world can satisfy, the most probable explanation is that I was made for another world."[9] We are not speaking of evil desires but desires that are good. Lewis further argues that joy is a signpost pointing to something transcendent and a reminder that joy can be satisfied in Christ. Christ satisfies our longings and desires because he is our true desire, our true joy.

Why do we desire to build things like AI to make society better? Why do we desire to *enhance* the body with technology, extend death, and strive for the eternal? Could the desire to develop AI and improve the world be a reminder and a signpost that a flourishing society can be achieved? The author of Ecclesiastes attests that God has set eternity in our hearts (Eccl 3:11). God has made humans distinct with knowledge, sensing that there is something more than just the here and now. For years, scientists have been developing medical advancements to *enhance* the body and extend life using AI. On a daily basis, marketers are offering to erase your wrinkles and improve your life with one superpower nutrient. Some of these suggestions could be beneficial, but the key point is that many are aimed at repairing the failing body. From birth, our bodies begin to age and ultimately die. "Transhumanism seeks to extend human life and ultimately overcome death, thereby transforming humans into posthumans. It seeks to improve human intelligence, physical strength, and the five senses by technological means."[10] Some people who seek to *enhance* the body and extend life beyond humanity's abilities seem to be attempting to attain the eternity God has placed in our hearts. Christianity claims there will be restoration and eternal life for Christians because Christ has already overcome death.

8. Lewis, *Surprised by Joy*, 89.

9. Lewis, *Mere Christianity*, 137.

10. Shatzer, *Transhumanism and the Image of God*, 40.

Christianity offers a better answer for eternal restoration than technology. These ideas will be further explored later in the chapter.

Although Christians understand that Christ will make all things new and suffering will cease to exist, today, we still live in the here and now. Christians have the responsibility to use the resources of creation faithfully. Encouraging and working toward being a good steward of creation resources is important. The perfect model to follow is Christ. You say, "But Christ did not have technology; yet he was a carpenter." He used the technology of the day and built various things. He demonstrated compassion and care for people for God's glory. People are made in the image of God, and they desire to help others who are sick and/or injured. With artificial intelligence (AI), new possibilities emerge for repair. We are witnessing some great discoveries, from repairing hearing loss with cochlear implants to heart patients using AI in pacemakers. The story of baby Aida stirred joy in most who watched her hear for the first time.[11] More recent surgeries use implants to help paralyzed people attain arm and leg movement.[12] Another example is Noland Arbaugh: after a spinal cord injury that left him paralyzed, Nolan received the first Neuralink brain chip, where his thoughts control his computer.[13] These repairs to the body are incredible. At the same time, people should think critically about the unintended consequences. Technology should encourage people to see the wonderful works of God. Typically, technology begins with the best of intentions. But Harai reminds us of what can happen with the example of plastic surgery:

> Modern plastic surgery was born in the First World War, when Harold Gillies began treating facial injuries in the Aldershot military hospital. When the war was over, surgeons discovered that the same techniques could also turn perfectly healthy but ugly noses into more beautiful specimens. Though plastic surgery continued to help the sick and wounded, it devoted increasing attention to upgrading the healthy. Nowadays plastic surgeons make millions in private clinics whose explicit and sole aim is to upgrade the healthy and beautify the wealthy.[14]

Plastic surgery has been a gift for repairing the body, but what about surgeries on the healthy? This should not imply that all plastic surgery is wrong

11. Williams, "Baby Hears for First Time."
12. Watt, "AI, Implants."
13. Lewington et al., Man with Mind-Reading Chip."
14. Noah Harari, *Homo Deus*, 61.

on healthy bodies, but it should cause us to pause and ask why we are having surgeries on healthy bodies. How far could the longings for the perfect take us in the age of biotechnology and biomedical engineering? Are the longings for the good, healthy, eternal life pointing to another world? How should we think about stewarding some of the discoveries?

The Enhancement Temptation

Voices call out to us regularly through work, media, friends, and family, urging us to live and act in specific ways. These voices include phrases that entice the hearer to buy or sell something, which could make life easier. Proverbs in the Bible remind readers that folly and wisdom call out for people to follow them. We must discern between the two.

> Wisdom shouts in the street,
> She lifts her voice in the square,
> At the head of the noisy streets she cries out. . . .
> 'Turn to my rebuke,
> Behold, I will pour out my spirit on you;
> I will make my words known to you.'" (Prov 1:20–23)

Folly also calls out, "She sits at the doorway of her house, on a seat by the high places of the city, calling to those who pass by" (Prov 9:14–15). These competing voices will always call out for our attention; one guides us in the path of righteousness, and the other guides us in the path of destruction. In the age of AI, it is imperative that Christians seek the principles of God's word, especially when making decisions, as the lines can easily get blurred. God desires his people to walk in righteousness because it brings about the best outcomes for our lives and those around us. But Satan has a different plan that produces destruction in our lives. He tempts and entices us by our own desires. Recall Gen 3:1, describing the serpent as "more crafty than any other beast of the field" (ESV). He set out to deceive Eve, luring her that his way was better. He does this by enticing her to question God's commands. He uses her desire to entice her into thinking that she can become wiser, as wise as God. Satan not only deceives Eve, but he is still on the move today, like a roaring lion, on the prowl, seeking someone to devour.

The desire to *enhance* healthy bodies and to overcome an earthly death is tempting. Remember, we encourage repairing the body to its original state, which may include the use of AI, surgeries, and other technologies connected to the body. Today's pacemakers are an excellent example of repair. The pacemaker is placed inside the heart to help regulate an irregular heartbeat and is connected to the internet for proper readings. However, we specifically caution healthy people against human *enhancement* methods that exceed the natural limits of the body. For example, Bryan Johnson has been at the forefront of using human *enhancement* methods. He is the leader of the Don't Die movement. A description on his website states, "We are a decentralized community united in defeating death and building prosperity."[15] Using vitamins and supplements to keep the body healthy is not the same as attempting to overcome death. In Johnson's documentary, he walks through all the supplements and *enhancements* he uses in his body to extend his life. Thousands of people have joined his movement. What is the appeal? It is people desiring to age well or end death altogether. People are drawn to the movement by their own desire to stay alive, but in the end, their allegiance is to their body. In the book of James, he provides a description of what it is like when humanity is tempted. James writes,

> When tempted, no one should say, "God is tempting me." For God cannot be tempted by evil, nor does he tempt anyone; but each person is tempted when they are dragged away by their own evil desire and enticed. Then, after desire has conceived, it gives birth to sin; and sin, when it is full-grown, gives birth to death. (Jas 1:13 NIV)

Some people attempting to experiment on their healthy body with numerous amounts of supplements and gene therapy to push the body beyond its natural limits may not realize it, but the body is dictating their life choices. Bryan Johnson is feeding a healthy body all sorts of pills and engaging in gene therapies, even to the point of spending $25,000 to participate in a follastatin gene therapy experiment to increase muscle mass and slow the aging process. His life focus is on overcoming death. It has been said "that sin will take you farther than you were willing to go, keep you longer than you were willing to stay, and cost you more than you were willing to pay."[16] We should be aware of the technological temptations that persuade us that the emerald city is beautiful and grand, when in reality they lead to illusions and false promises. We must be in prayer for discernment and the guidance of the Holy Spirit to avoid technological entrapments. Jesus advised his disciples to pray: "And lead us not into temptation, but deliver us from the evil one" (Matt 6:13 NIV).

15. See Bryan Johnson's home page: https://www.bryanjohnson.com/.

16. Widely attributed to Adrian Rogers. De Courcey, "It Comes at a Cost."

"There is nothing inherently wrong in living longer and healthier lives, and medicine should be celebrated as a good gift in achieving this worthwhile goal."[17] However, transhumanists aim to provide people with a better quality of life while aiming to overcome death. They would like to extend life, reduce suffering, and eradicate disease. Which sounds good on the surface, but at what cost? Many of them are proponents of embryonic stem cell research and therapeutic cloning. According to Brent Waters, the goal of transhumanism

> will be achieved initially by extending longevity through improved diets and healthcare employing regenerative medical techniques. More expansively, humans will gradually merge with their technology through the application of sophisticated prosthetics, employing anticipated developments in nanotechnology, artificial intelligence, and robotics.[18]

At first glance, these ideas appear to be beneficial, as they would seem to help alleviate suffering and extend life. Some of the technology will benefit humanity in many areas. However, the transhumanist movement aspires to achieve new heights in medicine; rather than relieving the human condition from suffering, it will attempt to transform it. CRISPR is an emerging technology that allows scientists to edit genes. They are able to modify, correct, and delete exact areas of a person's DNA. Gene editing will present many people with very difficult decisions. Gene editing is promoted to cure diseases and prevent various illnesses. Doctors are already able to help people with diseases. For instance, KJ was born with a rare genetic disease at the Children's Hospital in Philadelphia in 2024. After birth, he spent several months in the hospital. He was eventually treated with customized gene therapy using CRISPR in February 2025, and now he is thriving.[19] This is a breakthrough in helping people overcome genetic disease. Yet, there are significant ethical concerns being raised regarding CRISPR. What are the long-term effects of altering DNA? Will humans become lab rats? What happens when transhumanists or others begin to use CRISPR for more than eradicating disease? The temptation to be *enhanced* could be before us. What if parents begin wanting to edit their kids' genes so they will have certain qualities? Who gets access to the treatment? Will they be able to create superhumans? Will humans with limitations be

17. Waters, *This Mortal Flesh*, 87.
18. Waters, *This Mortal Flesh*, 97.
19. Children's Hospital of Philadelphia, "World's First Patient."

devalued? Will it cause inequality? These are the ethical questions that are raised when attempting to perfect humanity.

Wisdom When Tempted

Today, we face numerous temptations with the AI advancements in biotechnology and biomedical engineering. It is imperative that people engage in discussions and raise questions about the ethical issues we encounter when using this technology. We are not saying we can't or shouldn't use it, but we should be discerning and keep in mind that Adam and Eve did not overcome the desire to be "like gods." They ate the fruit, and sin and death entered the world. The temptation before them was luring them to be more than what they were made to be. Their failure to stand firm against that temptation ultimately led to death, as Adam and Eve rejected their limitations.

Limitations need not be perceived as a negative but as something God granted us for the good of humanity and society. Something as simple as needing sleep after staying awake for long periods of time to work on projects or needing rest after hanging out for an evening with friends. People need sleep for their bodies, and it is a natural restorer. Therefore, the body's natural limitations drive people to rest. But often, society praises people for efficiency and productivity rather than for who they are as a person. Rest is sometimes equated with laziness because production has stopped. People are tempted to fill every minute with activity, even at their own detriment. But rest restores and allows people time to cultivate relationships. This does not imply that people should be lazy but instead that God has made man with limits. Humanity belongs to God, and his creation limits are good. Alan Noble discusses the idea that man does not belong to himself in the book *You Are Not Your Own*. He writes about how many in modern life are attempting to forge their own identity. He writes, "We've created a society based on the assumption that we are our own and belong to ourselves."[20] He further explains that people, apart from God, seeking their own unquenchable desires, make humanity worse off. He writes, "Autonomy sounds comforting, and freedom is valorized by society as one of the highest goods, but in practice freedom without limits is a kind of hell . . . which takes many forms."[21] The transhumanists' quest to make their own way and push past the limits of earthly death is a futile ambition.

20. Noble, *You Are Not Your Own*, 18

21. Noble, *You Are Not Your Own*, 198.

But there is a second temptation in the Bible that gives us hope. It happened in the wilderness, shortly after Jesus was baptized. Just like Adam and Eve, Satan emerges to tempt Jesus to serve him rather than God. He tempts him when he is fasting in the desert. Jesus is hungry. Instead of failing God, Jesus is obedient and faithful. The event unfolds in Matt 4:3–11. Jesus is not just tempted once, but he is tempted three times by Satan:

1. "And the tempter came and said to Him, 'If You are the Son of God, command that these stones become bread.' But He answered and said,'It is written, Man shall not live on bread alone, but on every word that proceeds out of the mouth of God'" (Matt 4:3–4).
2. "Then the devil took Him into the holy city and had Him stand on the pinnacle of the temple, and said to Him, 'If You are the Son of God, throw Yourself down; for it is written, "He will command His angels concerning You; and On *their* hands they will bear You up, So that You will not strike Your foot against a stone."' Jesus said to him,'On the other hand, it is written, You shall not put the Lord your God to the test'" (Matt 4:5–7).
3. "Again, the devil took Him to a very high mountain and showed Him all the kingdoms of the world and their glory; and he said to Him, 'All these things I will give You, if You fall down and worship me.' Then Jesus said to him,'Go, Satan! For it is written, You shall worship the Lord your God, and serve Him only'" (Matt 4:8–10).

Satan tempted Jesus when he was most hungry. This is what the enemy does. Proverbs 27:7 warns us that "one who is full loathes honey from the comb, but to the hungry even what is bitter tastes sweet." When someone is searching for answers to their problems, they can be entrapped by false promises. Satan tempts us with power, rulership, and material things. He promises that he can offer a better life than God. Just like with the wilderness temptations, Satan knew that Jesus had the power to turn the stones into bread. But Jesus knew that God's word was the greatest way forward. Satan wanted Jesus to worship him, and in return, Satan offered the world. We will be tempted in many ways by the new advancements AI is bringing to technology. But remember God's word: "No temptation has overtaken you except what is common to mankind. And God is faithful; he will not let you be tempted beyond what you can bear. But when you are tempted, he will also provide a way out so that you can endure it" (1 Cor 10:13 NIV).

The temptations to upgrade the body will be alluring. It seems exaggerated that people will want to merge technology with healthy bodies. Eventually, they could become cyborgs, being part human and part machine. Biohacking can be translated as "do-it-yourself biology." It is becoming the future of personal wellness. Biohackers are using science and technology to optimize physical well-being. They are experimenting with their bodies, seeking enhancements that will extend their abilities and health. In 2019, "biohacker Michael Laufer had a 512 GB drive implanted in his leg, which can store data, stream music or movies, and power a hot spot and mesh network. It's called the PegLeg."[22] He is healthy and has never had surgery before the PegLeg surgery. But why put something in the body if you can access those things outside the body? Laufer says, "A wearable can be confiscated at the border, a wearable has to have an internal power source that will fail . . . having it in the body, part of the magic is that no one can force me to turn it on."[23] Laufer is one of the boldest biohackers; he is in what is known as the "grinding community," on the cutting edge of biohacking. He mentions people using night vision eye drops and flexible armor implants that are pushing the body beyond its limits. The temptation for upgrades will become more and more common. As mentioned earlier, plastic surgery that started out as a help to injured people in wars, fires, and accidents soon became a billion-dollar industry among the healthy.

Remember, the temptations of today may seem new, but they are age-old invitations to exceed our human capacity. Adam and Eve fell prey to the deceiver's call to become "like gods." However, Jesus demonstrated that through God's word, we can gain wisdom to battle against Satan's temptations. As a society, we face the challenge of *enhancing* our healthy bodies. As Christians, let us point to the guiding principles of what it means to order our loves correctly, making decisions that will glorify God rather than man.

STEWARDING TECHNOLOGY WITH REORDERED LOVES

Disordered Loves

When Adam and Eve sought to "become like gods," their lives became disordered. They abandoned the first chief good, which is to love and glorify God. Yet, they chose to love the idea of gaining knowledge and pleasing self.

22. Oberhaus, "Biohacker Explains," para. 1.

23. Oberhaus, "Biohacker Explains," 4:04.

As a result, their loves became disordered. The prophet Jeremiah wrote to the people of Judah when they had turned their backs on God's provision:

> For My people have committed two evils:
> They have forsaken Me,
> The fountain of living waters,
> To hew for themselves cisterns,
> Broken cisterns
> That can hold no water. (Jer 2:13)

Disordering our loves causes us to seek things that seem pleasing for a moment but, in the end, bite like a snake.

David Naugle wrote, "Ignorance and disordered love are two of the primary consequences of humanity's fall into sin."[24] Both ignorance and disordered love are reasons that complicate decision-making when considering the merging of technology and humanity. The question is, who is controlling our hearts as we are attempting to steward technology in our society? Naugle writes,

> Disordered love isn't really love at all when in our diseased hearts it becomes demonic in its demands. If God's love for us and our love for God do not control us, then who knows what we might say or do to ensure our self-preservation and to satisfy our mental needs and bodily obsessions, especially since our sense of peace and purpose are dependent upon them.[25]

Our disordered loves do and will continue to cause disordered lives.

If we have disordered loves, then we will have disordered thinking. Therefore, when people hear persuasive arguments about achieving a better life through upgrades, it could be another false promise from the enemy, suggesting that a healthier and happier society is possible if we surrender our minds and bodies to the wisdom of science. Science itself, of course, is not bad, but when science pushes the body beyond its natural limits, is it really better?

If the purpose and focus of life is eradicating sickness and suffering, then we may be left in a sea of disappointment in the end. We live in a world where the enemy is the god of this world for a time, seeking to deceive people with promises that will not last. Second Corinthians 4:4 says, "The god of this world has blinded the minds of the unbelieving so that they

24. Naugle, *Reordered Love, Reordered Lives*, 62.

25. Naugle, *Reordered Love, Reordered Lives*, 31.

might not see the light of the gospel of the glory of Christ, who is the image of God." Augustine says,

> We see then that there are two cities created by two kinds of love: the earthly city was created by self-love reaching the point of contempt for God. The Heavenly City by the love of God carried as far as contempt of self. In fact, the earthly city glories in itself; the Heavenly City glories in the Lord. The former looks for glory from men, the latter finds its highest glory in God.[26]

Understanding that people have disordered loves can help us in conversations with people about these advancing technologies. It appears that transhumanists, who aim to move humanity into the posthuman stage, are ultimately pursuing a fruitless endeavor. Psalm 4:2 asks a thoughtful question: "How long will you love what is worthless and aim at deception?" Yet, there is hope to reorder our loves and be on a path that uses technology for the glory of God.

Reordered Love

John the apostle reminds us that "the thief comes only to steal and kill and destroy, but Jesus came that we may have life, and have it abundantly" (John 10:10). Jesus Christ stood against the temptations of Satan and walked a sinless life. He was crucified, buried, and on the third day, he rose from the dead, overcoming death. John says, "Jesus first loved us in that while we were sinners, Christ died for us" (1 John 4:10). Jesus is the path out of the earthly city, and he is the way into the Heavenly City. When we turn from our sin and turn to Christ, he gives us the Holy Spirit that will guide us in all truth. Our hearts are renewed and reordered by Christ. Our minds are renewed by the word of God.

Our reordered loves compel us to conform to the image of Christ. As we grow in our Christian faith, we develop the fruit of the Spirit. Bearing fruit of love, joy, peace, patience, kindness, goodness, faithfulness, gentleness, and self-control. We grow in what it means to love one another. We are to seek good for one another. Growing in love, having the Holy Spirit, the mind of Christ, and the fruit of the Spirit, we are enabled to be discerning in the technology before us. Christians are also able to have compassion on people who desire good ways of helping people but may be misled by the

26. Augustine, *City of God*, 593.

temptations of this world. It is an opportunity to have robust conversations about *enhancements* and futuristic modifications to the body.

While transhumanists are looking for ways to conquer death, Christ has already overcome death. It is because he lives that those who place their trust in him will also live. The fear of dying can be removed. The fear of being unable to perform like a superhero can be removed. God created humanity with limitations. Social media has opened up visibility to see thousands of lives in real-time, and people are often decrying their limitations due to constant comparison. People are willing to go to extreme measures to keep up. But God created each individual with different gifts and talents. We were not all born to run fast or type well. We are created to express our particular gifts to glorify God. Losing sight of knowing and pleasing God can lead us to think that we do need to be superhuman to keep up.

Reasons for Caution in Biotechnology/Biomedical Engineering

One of the main reasons we should have concern is that we live in a fallen world. If we begin to say that something is good for humanity, then where is the standard to measure that good? The standard of good is God. He is the objective standard by which we measure all things. If a person is a nonbeliever, then what boundary lines are they using? Technology can help repair humanity, but where are the guardrails to prevent people from becoming experiments? Humans have been able to mitigate suffering to some degree, for instance, Yuval Harari claims, "For the first time in history, more people will die today from eating too much than from eating too little, and more people will die from old age than from infectious diseases."[27] Yes, technological advancements have extended life. But alarm bells should be ringing when considering merging technology with humanity for the healthy, because we live in a fallen world, and humans, apart from God, will lack boundaries when experimenting on themselves or others.

Brent Waters describes people who desire to advance posthumanism and points out that some have hesitations. A critic of the core beliefs of transhumanism, Katherine Hayles believes that the future of technology and humanity joining is inevitable but that modern anthropology and technoscience will prove problematic, ultimately, because "the end result is that persons are reduced to little more than assertive wills expressed through

27. Harari, *Homo Deus*, 2.

various biological and silicon-based prosthetics."[28] Therefore, limits should be placed on the ability of humans to employ technology to transform themselves.

A second concern is that humans will become experiments. They could be viewed as only matter that is here to advance people into the post-human era. But what limits will be guardrails preventing humanity from reducing people to machines? The biohackers and grinding community are found conducting experiments outside of institutions. They are more autonomous and willing to experiment with trials on themselves. It will be the everyday awareness and conversations that bring these things to light.

A third concern is the devaluing of human dignity. Valuing humans for simply being human will begin to fade with each person's upgrades. People could begin to loathe their body and who they are as a person. Many will learn to base their value on their performance rather than simply being made in the image of God (more in the next section on that).

The fourth concern will be the idea that we can overcome death. We learned earlier that eternity has been set in our hearts by God. Each individual will die and live in an eternal state, either with God or apart from him. But to have a movement that strives to prevent death in this earthly city implies that death should not happen to the point that it is our job to prevent it. It is terrible to lose a loved one, but if they are a believer, the Bible says that to be absent from the body is to be present with the Lord.[29] To be present with the Lord, there is no more suffering, and there is life eternal with God. It is good to be alive and grow in God while we are in the earthly city. We can enjoy family and friends, but there is a greater city to come, the Heavenly City. Our striving should not be to overcome death; Christ has already done that. We should be focused on loving God and loving our neighbor. The task to overcome death is too much for humanity to bear.

Lastly, the fifth concern is the diminishing of human equality. As humans merge with technology, becoming stronger and faster and living longer, who will receive the upgrades? What happens to people without upgrades? Designing children through gene editing could also impact human equality by elevating the ability to shape human beings in one's likeness. Of course, this will trap the child into a life created by the parents.

The concerns exceed the following that have been discussed, but they are no less.

28. Waters, *This Mortal Flesh*, 98.

29. 2 Cor 5:8.

1. Humanity exists in a fallen world, and we need boundary lines.
2. Humans can be reduced to trial experiments and machines.
3. Humans made in the image of God will disappear along with human dignity.
4. Humans will learn to fear dying.
5. Human equality will diminish.

WHAT DOES IT MEAN TO BE HUMAN?

Made in the Image of God

The distinction of God's image on humanity sets them apart from the rest of creation. Every human is made in the image of God, and this places inherent value and dignity on every individual. The psalmist says it well in Ps 8:3–8:

> When I consider Your heavens, the work of Your fingers,
> The moon and the stars, which You have ordained;
> What is man that You take thought of him,
> And the son of man that You care for him?
> Yet You have made him a little lower than God,
> And You crown him with glory and majesty!
> You make him to rule over the works of Your hands;
> You have put all things under his feet,
> All sheep and oxen,
> And also the beasts of the field,
> The birds of the heavens and the fish of the sea,
> Whatever passes through the paths of the seas.

Humans inherently have value because we are made in the image of God. We don't have to be superhuman to have value. We don't have to be free from all disease to have value. We have value simply because we are made in the image of God. But what does that mean? There are three popular theories: functional, relational, and structural. Some people may choose one theory over another, or they may accept a combination of all three.[30]

30. Deanna Huff, "The *Imago Dei*, Animals, and Transhumanism," in Chilton, *Why Creationism Still Matters*, 137.

Functional Theory

The functional view has had a long-standing history in traditional Christian circles. It consists of what a person does. Adam and Eve were created to be functional, meaning they were commanded to have dominion over the earth, work it, and care for it. They were given vice-regency positions with the intention that God's children would use their delegated authority to care for the world. They were meant to worship and serve God. The functional theory entails utilizing and taking responsibility for all the resources of the created order for the glory of God and the good of others.

The functional view of the image of God "attempts to determine from the biblical text itself the content of the image . . . 'let us make mankind in our image, in our likeness' is followed immediately by 'so that they may rule over the fish of the sea.'"[31] It is recognized that this is the command of work and how humanity is to function; they have dominion over the animals and land.

Structural Theory

Another view of the image of God is the structural theory. Humans are sapient beings, referring to the human capacity for rational thought. God has rational thought, and humans imitate it in some sense. People are thinking beings with the ability to have knowledge, evaluate evidence, and make informed decisions. Humans have a sense of morality, recognizing right and wrong. They strive for human achievement.

There is something about how God created the minds and bodies of humans that distinguishes them from the rest of creation—mind, will, and consciousness—that sets man apart. Two observations sum up the unique rationale of man. First, they are sapient beings marked by a level of cognition and intelligence. Sapient beings are knowledgeable and self-aware. Secondly, they provide a picture of human progress through the use of their knowledge and their cultural advancements.

Relational Theory

In the relational view, humans have vertical and horizontal relationships. Vertically, they can have a spiritual relationship with God, and horizontally, they share relationships with people. They are fundamentally relational in

31. Erickson, *Christian Theology*, 466.

this world. Some would espouse that the relational view reflects the Trinity, being that God is in continual relationship with the three persons of the Godhead. The connection ties to the divine plurality in Gen 1:26, which says, "Let us make man in Our image." Genesis 1:28 states, "God said to them," signifying he had a relationship with both Adam and Eve, and they had a relationship with one another. Yet, the deterioration of these relationships is the effect of sin in the world. Still, relationships collaborating together remain a cornerstone in society.

In the three aforementioned views, some people may use counterarguments to state their disagreement with a particular image of God theory. Some may raise questions regarding the functional view, such as individuals who are born with limitations that prevent them from ruling, such as being blind and deaf. These exceptions to the rule reveal that in the fall of mankind, disease and suffering entered the world. Yet, people were meant to fulfill their full potential, but the curse of sin manifests in different ways that limit their full potential. However, God's image is still in man and is note, "Whoever sheds man's blood, By man his blood shall be shed, For in the image of God He made man" (Gen 9:6). Others may counter the structural theory by providing examples of humans lacking acute rational capacities, such as human embryos or Alzheimer's patients who either have never possessed or have significantly lost rational functions. They ask, "Are they human persons on those accounts?"[32]

In both instances, the structural potential is present, but it is underdeveloped or impaired, and the potential for rationality is also present. One day, this will be restored either through a repair or in heaven.

In summary of the three views of the image of God, it seems best to take the combined approach of all three. The reader can adhere to only one view, but it will be insufficient and restrictive. Although there may be a lack of information to fully comprehend what it means for humans to bear God's image, the information provided in the Bible is sufficient to identify humanity as the pinnacle of the species.

Eternal Soul

Humans are not only functional, structural, and relational, they are also material and immaterial beings having an eternal soul as written about in chapter 1. The Bible reveals that "God formed man of dust from the ground

32. Mitchell, "What It Means," 75.

and breathed into his nostrils the breath of life; and the man became a living person" (Gen 2:7). In Ecclesiastes, the preacher writes, "Then the dust will return to the earth as it was, and the spirit will return to God who gave it" (Eccl 12:7). In the New Testament, Matthew writes, "Do not be afraid of those who kill the body but are unable to kill the soul; but rather fear Him who is able to destroy both soul and body in hell" (Matt 10:28). There is also Paul, who speaks of being absent from the body and being home with the Lord (2 Cor 5:8). The human body can die, but the soul will live into eternity.

Christ

Humans are made in God's image, but Christ is the exact image of God. John Kilner attests, "Humanity and Christ both have a special connection with God. However, there are important differences between them."[33] Man is made in the likeness of God, whereas Jesus Christ is God.

This is observed in Colossians, where Paul presents Jesus' identity. Referring to Christ, Col 1:15 states, "He is the image of the invisible God, the firstborn of all creation." G. K. Beale states, "Col 1:15 refers not to Christ as the 'image' in his human incarnational and exalted form. Rather, as is in verses 15b–17, Christ's preexistence as God's divine 'image' is the focus, though his status as the divine image still applies to his incarnational state and eternal exalted status."[34] He did not become the image of God at his incarnation, but he is the image of God before all things were made. He is the exact imprint of God. When you see him, you have seen the Father (John 14:9). Jesus is God in the flesh.

The invisible God becomes visible in Christ. In Heb 1:3, it states that the Son is the radiance of God's glory and the exact representation of his being. Through the redemption of Christ, humanity is being renewed in the mind by putting off the old self and putting on the new self, as described in Eph 4:22–26. Although sin hindered humanity from fully displaying the likeness of God, no human person can lose the image of God. Believers can conform to the likeness of God by following Christ. When Jesus returns, there will be a further transformation known as glorification. John states, "Beloved, now we are children of God, and it has not appeared as yet what

33. Kilner, *Dignity and Destiny*, 59.

34. Beale et al., *Colossians and Philemon*, 269.

we will be. We know that when He appears, we will be like Him because we will see Him just as He is" (1 John 3:2).

God Heals People

The Bible specifies that God is healer. From the beginning pages, Exod 15:26 states, "For I am the LORD who heals you." Psalm 103:3 states, "Who forgives all your iniquities, Who heals all your diseases." In Jer 30:17, God promises, "But I will restore you to health and heal your wounds." He loves his creation and desires for suffering to end, and this is the beautiful unfolding of God redeeming humanity through Christ. For all who come to Him, they will live in the afterlife with Him, where suffering is no more.

When the incarnate Christ Jesus arrived, He performed many miracles to demonstrate His deity. He had compassion for the people. He opened the eyes of the blind. He opened the ears of the deaf. He raised the dead. Jesus, like His Father healed the sick and cured diseases. Therefore, it is no surprise that people desire to help other people out of their suffering. Yet, there is one important observation with Jesus. There were never miracles where he *enhanced* the body for people. He did not make them faster or stronger to exceed the natural limits of the body. He repaired them back to their normal health.

God Gives Life Eternal

God is the creator of the world and the giver of life. He has the power and goodness to perfectly create humanity. Isaiah 42:5 states,

> Thus says God the Lord,
> Who created the heavens and stretched them out,
> Who spread out the earth and its offspring,
> Who gives breath to the people on it.

When Adam and Eve sinned in the garden, God did not allow them to eat from the tree of life because he didn't want them to remain in their sin in this earthly city. Instead, God removed them from the garden, sent Jesus to save humanity, and will one day call his followers to be in the new heavens and new earth.

However, transhumanists want to extend life in the fallen world for people. This reminds me of the Greek mythology when King Sisyphus was punished by the gods for his deceit and pride. The gods eternally punished him in the underworld by having him roll a massive boulder up a hill, only for it to roll back down every time he neared the top. He was forced to repeat the task forever. This futile labor was never ending. Imagine being on earth forever in its sinful state. The suffering and the pain would always emerge some how, some way. Even if humanity thinks they can conquer death, people would still live in a fallen world. But Christ came that we might have life and have it abundantly. In this life we can have peace in Christ but Jesus is returning for his people. Revelation 21:2–4 describes the new heavenly city,

> And I saw the holy city, new Jerusalem, coming down out of heaven from God, made ready as a bride adorned for her husband. And I heard a loud voice from the throne, saying, "Behold, the tabernacle of God is among men, and He will dwell among them, and they shall be His people, and God Himself will be among them, and He will wipe away every tear from their eyes; and there will no longer be *any* death; there will no longer be *any* mourning, or crying, or pain; the first things have passed away."

CONCLUSION

Furthermore, advancements in human *enhancement* will continue to call, prompting people to upgrade their bodies. Transhumanists will continue to offer solutions to build the body in better ways and extend life even to the point of trying to overcome death. Will the church be ready to respond? Remember, we have seen these temptations before, maybe in a different shape or format, but the promise is to be beyond what we are made to be. Will we be able to share how Christ responded to the temptations? Will we share what it means to be human and let those principles guide difficult decisions in the future? As Christians, we can show people that there is an objective standard of good in God. When discussing technology, we must remember to share the importance of valuing all individuals. God is the giver of life, and he allows us to benefit from wonderful medical technologies that repair the body. But, will we be satisfied with merely repairing the body, or will society seek to develop people to merge with technology and travel beyond their limits? God offers a better way; his way offers an eternal resurrected life with no more suffering and no more pain. It is a life of joy beyond all measure. Christianity offers the way to a righteous, reordered, and eternal life. Which path will humanity take?

CHAPTER QUESTIONS AND CONVERSATION STARTERS

1. Define your terms. What is *enhancement* vs. *repair*?
2. What was the temptation that caused Adam and Eve to rebel against God?
3. What were the temptations offered to Jesus?
4. What are the temptations offered in our society by transhumanists?
5. How does understanding what it means to be human and havng limitations help us with ethical discussions?
6. Who gives eternal life?
7. How can the ideas of merging technology with humanity be a bridge to the gospel?

BIBLIOGRAPHY

Augustine. *City of God*. Translated by Henry Bettenson. London: Penguin, 2003.

Beale, G. K., et al. *Colossians and Philemon*. Baker Exegetical Commentary on the New Testament. Grand Rapids: Baker Academic, 2019.

Bostrom, Nick. "Transhumanist Values." https://nickbostrom.com/ethics/values.

Children's Hospital of Philadelphia. "World's First Patient Treated with Personalized CRISPR Gene Editing Therapy at Children's Hospital of Philadelphia." May 15, 2025. https://www.chop.edu/news/worlds-first-patient-treated-personalized-crispr-gene-editing-therapy-childrens-hospital.

Chilton, Brian G., et al., eds. *Why Creationism Still Matters*. West Frankfort, IL: IHP Nexus, 2024.

De Courcey, Philip. "It Comes at a Cost." Know the Truth, Apr. 5, 2024. https://ktt.org/so-true-devotional/it-comes-at-a-cost.

Erickson, Millard J. *Christian Theology*. Grand Rapids: Baker Academic, 2013.

Harari, Yuval Noah. *Homo Deus: A Brief History of Tomorrow*. London: Penguin Random House, 2015.

Humanity Plus. "Our Mission." https://www.humanityplus.org/about.

Juengst, Eric, and Daniel Moseley. "Human Enhancement." Stanford Encyclopedia of Philosophy, May 15, 2019. https://plato.stanford.edu/archives/spr2025/entries/enhancement/#Ter.

Kilner, John F. *Dignity and Destiny: Humanity in the Image of God*. Grand Rapids: Eerdmans, 2015.

Lewington, Lara, et al. "The Man with a Mind-Reading Chip in His Brain—Thanks to Elon Musk." BBC News, Mar. 22, 2025. https://www.bbc.com/news/articles/cewk49j7j1po.

Lewis, C. S. *Mere Christianity*. London: William Collins, 1952.

———. *Surprised by Joy*. London: William Collins, 1955.

Mitchell, C. Ben. "What It Means to Be Human." In *Created in the Image of God: Applications and Implications for Our Cultural Confusion*, edited by David S. Dockery and Lauren McAfee, 69–84. Nashville: Forefront, 2023.

Naugle, David K. *Reordered Love, Reordered Lives: Learning the Deep Meaning of Happiness*. Grand Rapids: Eerdmans, 2008.

Noble, Alan. *You Are Not Your Own: Belonging to God in an Inhuman World*. Downers Grove, IL: InterVarsity, 2021.

Oberhaus, Daniel. "A Biohacker Explains Why He Turned His Leg Into a Hotspot." Wired, Aug. 30, 2019. https://www.wired.com/video/watch/a-biohacker-explains-why-he-turned-his-leg-into-a-hotspot.

Shatzer, Jacob. *Transhumanism and the Image of God: Today's Technology and the Future of Christian Discipleship*. Downers Grove, IL: IVP Academic, 2019.

Waters, Brent. *This Mortal Flesh: Incarnation and Bioethics*. Grand Rapids: Brazos, 2009.

Watt, Nick. "AI, Implants Form 'Digital Bridge' to Help Paralyzed Man Move Arms, Hands." CNN, Sept. 27, 2023. https://www.cnn.com/2023/09/27/health/digital-bridge-implants-paralysis/index.html.

Williams, Vivian. "Baby Hears for First Time with Cochlear Implants." News Network Mayo Clinic, Nov. 13, 2018. https://newsnetwork.mayoclinic.org/discussion/baby-hears-for-first-time-with-cochlear-implants/.

6

Stewarding Social Media, Chatbots, and Community

Deanna Huff, PhD

The agnostic technocrat thinks that he must shove God aside for technology to flourish. The Christian agrarian thinks that he must shove technology aside in order for faith to thrive. But both the tech optimist and the tech pessimist sell God short.[1]

—Tony Reinke

People were made for community. This is why it is not surprising that people enjoy connecting on social and professional media platforms. The establishment of LinkedIn in 2003, Facebook in 2004, Twitter in 2006 (which later became X in 2024), and Instagram in 2010 had the hopes of creating spaces where people could connect. There are fabulous stories about the benefits of social media and chatbots as well as horror stories, and it seems we have three options for dealing with them. We can retreat from all social media and chatbots. We can misuse and participate without guardrails. Or we can apply the guidelines of Scripture, participate, and lead the way in

1. Reinke, *God, Technology, and Christian Life*, 29.

stewarding AI, social media, and chatbots. This does not mean that we will not falter at times; we are human, and at times, we will fail, but it does mean that God has provided principles in the Bible to guide us in how we use technology and treat others. Humanity has a moral responsibility, but machines are not human and do not carry a moral responsibility. Therefore, it is up to humanity to steward AI technology. The positive and negative aspects of AI, social media, and chatbots are before society; the church can pave the way forward if we steward them well and influence others to follow.

Many people using social media are attempting to connect with friends and family and to discover what is happening in the world around them. People using chatbots typically receive helpful answers to their questions, and companies are leveraging the bots to improve their business operations. AI is here, and we need not fear it; instead, we should learn how to steward it well. Will people misuse AI? Yes, just like there are people who misuse knives in the kitchen. People can use knives for cooking and slicing fresh bread, or they can use knives to harm others. We need wisdom in the ways we use technology. In the book *God, Technology, and the Christian Life*, Tony Reinke says,

> God created the earth, and he called it good. He shot electricity through the sky, scattered uranium deposits inside the soil, and stuffed genetic codes into cells. . . . All of this technology was intended to be discovered. . . . We have been entrusted with explosive powers. . . . We wield powers that require great diligence and wisdom.[2]

All technology that is discovered comes with both positive and negative aspects. Reinke makes the point that when a person digs a pit, he can also fall into it. When ships are created, shipwrecks are also created.[3] As mentioned in previous chapters, we live under the fall of Adam and Eve. The new AI technology offers many benefits, but it also has drawbacks. Therefore, we can encourage the positive AI technologies and use wisdom to mitigate their negative aspects. Christians have the opportunity to influence society by using our resources well, if and when we submit to the Holy Spirit, who guides us in all truth.

One of the necessary elements of using AI technology involves moral responsibility. Mark Coeckelbergh states,

2. Reinke, *God, Technology, and Christian Life*, 128.
3. Reinke, *God, Technology, and Christian Life*, 134.

> When AI is used to make decisions for us and to do things for us, we encounter a problem that is shared with all automation technologies but which becomes even more important when AI enables us to delegate far more to machines than we used to: responsibility attribution. If AI is given more agency and takes over what humans used to do, how do we then attribute moral responsibility? Who is responsible for the harms and benefits of the technology when humans delegate agency and decisions to AI? To put it in terms of risk: who is responsible when something goes wrong?[4]

Technology will always let humanity down to some degree, and these are some of the negatives that humans will have to face with AI technology. We are in a fallen world, and it will never be our savior. Even ancient people have trusted in their technology at times. Psalm 20:7 says, "Some trust in chariots and some in horses, but we trust in the name of the Lord our God." But the beginning of wisdom is the fear of the Lord. We should understand that he is sovereign over everything and he created all things. People will face positive and negative aspects of AI technology, and as a society, we must learn how to steward it well.

THERE ARE POSITIVE AND NEGATIVE ASPECTS

Positive Aspects of Social Media

The positive aspects of social media allow people to connect and share their lives, even though distance prevents regular gatherings. For example, my brothers live a state away from me, yet I often get to see pictures of my nieces and nephews in their school activities, fun adventures, and family outings. When I do get the wonderful opportunity to see them in person, I get to encourage them in their activities. In addition, when COVID shut down the world in 2020, I was able to watch church services online and visit with my fellow church members through the social media feeds when I could not attend in person. Social media also allows you to congratulate people or wish them a happy birthday. There have been many times when friends have provided updates on sick patients for prayer requests, which remind me to take time to pray for their families. There have been emergency broadcasts that have helped families locate loved ones.

4. Coeckelbergh, *AI Ethics*, 109.

Then there is the sharing of biblical education and encouragement. There are thousands of Christian communities creating social media content that aim to grow people in their faith and love for God. Some websites create content to educate people in the faith. For example, I work with Bellator Christi, a journal that creates content to help people defend Christianity. That content is published and circulated through several social media platforms to make people aware that they can access these articles. Many churches use social media to post podcasts and sermons. Social media can raise awareness of great Christian books. While social media has its positive aspects, there are always negative aspects we need to keep in mind.

Negative Aspects of Social Media

One of the concerns of social media is self-indulgence. Indulging is often promoted over self-control in our society. Denying yourself, self-discipline, and restraint are words some people would rather avoid. Yet self-control is needed in all areas of life. From the beginning pages of Scripture, Cain is warned in Gen 4:7: "Sin is crouching at the door. Its desire is for you, and you must rule over it." He was warned by God about his anger, and God instructed him to master it, but instead, he gave full vent to his anger and killed his brother Abel. It is through a relationship with Jesus Christ that we receive the Holy Spirit, which enables us to walk in the Spirit and exercise self-control.

There is a significant point to mention regarding the development of kids on social media vs. adults. Jonathan Haidt wrote in *The Anxious Generation* that the frontal cortex in minors is essential for self-control, but it is not at full capacity until the mid-20s. He says, "As they begin puberty, they are often socially insecure, easily swayed by peer pressure, and easily lured by any activity that seems to offer social validation."[5] With the AI technology in social media, it learns what resonates with a person by their pauses and clicks on information. AI enables the algorithms to tailor to the taste of the user. Haidt mentions that designers of social media platforms install triggers that automatically ping the phone in an effort to hook the students to the social media platform. It is easy for kids and adults to end up scrolling for hours. Haidt encourages parents to avoid giving kids smartphones before age fourteen and keep social media away until age sixteen. In

5. Haidt, *Anxious Generation*, 5.

addition, he encourages phone-free schools so they can give teachers their attention. When there are no guardrails from parents, kids go off track.

Parents are decrying that their kids are becoming addicted to their phones. The *New York Post* recently ran a story titled "Parents Frantic to Shield Teens from 'Addictive' Screen Time Are Turning to 'Detox' Camps and Even Other Tech." These parents are expressing their frustration with their teens, who are unable to detach from their phones. The article states, "This time away from home for minors aged 13 to 18 is meant to help children with everything from social anxiety to depression to gaming and social media addiction."[6] It is important that adults have self-control, and parents must set the example for their children while establishing guardrails when the kids cannot. Sometimes people have jobs that keep them on social media regularly. Screen time may look different for everyone. It is through self-control that people can use technology wisely.

Loneliness is a second concern regarding social media. Connecting people online was never meant to replace people gathering in person for fellowship and friendship. Online friendships can't replace offline friendships, especially for children. "Digital technologies offer boundless avenues for connection, but cannot fully replace the face-to-face interactions vital to children's social development . . . former U.S. surgeon general warned that the loneliness epidemic is hitting adolescents especially hard."[7] Loneliness affects children, but it also affects adults in enormous ways.

Loneliness is a result of the fall. Although it is clear that God said it was not good for man to be alone, he was stating a fact, not expressing an emotion Adam felt. God created Eve, which began the community of family and fellowship with humans. It was the fall of Adam and Eve that destroyed the perfect relationship with God and one another. God created us to have fellowship with one another; however, sin has destroyed that perfectness, leaving sin, shame, blame, rejection, and other ingredients that perpetuate feelings of loneliness. One may look at Genesis and only see the image of marriage as fulfilling loneliness; however, this is not the case. Yes, God did institute marriage in Genesis because marriage honors God and grows Christian communities. But Paul wrote in 1 Cor 7 that both marriage and singleness can honor God. Both are good when our lives are seeking to glorify God. But the emphasis here is that the church community is something God provided to help encourage followers of Christ. Matthew

6. Lax, "Frantic Parents," para. 3.

7. Andoh, "Many Teens Are Turning," para. 11.

12:48–50 reveals where Jesus enlarges and redefines the community of family that provides the fellowship every believer needs: Jesus says, "'Who is my mother, and who are my brothers?' And stretching out his hand toward his disciples, he said, 'Here are my mother and my brothers! For whoever does the will of my Father in heaven is my brother and sister and mother'" (ESV).

And later in Revelation, when Christ returns, people are in community as a bride to Christ, not one to another. Therefore, we can see from Scripture that restoration with Christ grants followers of Christ a new community that is meant to edify believers. At the same time, one must realize that the fullness of loneliness will not be completely eliminated until heaven, but for now, he has given the church to provide fellowship and community. This community is more than people relating to one another on Sunday; it is God's family, and all believers are brothers and sisters. This community, though it sometimes faces challenges due to sin, will more often provide love, prayer, and encouragement for one another in the darkest times.

An additional concern regarding social media on smartphones is the constant distraction posed by these apps. It happens with adults and teens. Regarding young people, Jonathan Haidt wrote, "The average number of notifications on young people's phones from the top social and communication apps amounts to 192 alerts per day. The average teen, who now gets only seven hours of sleep per night, therefore gets about 11 notifications per waking hour, or one every five minutes."[8] Adults also have to deal with phone apps calling out through notifications. For many people, they are fighting the battle to stay focused and on task. Instead, they sometimes get distracted by notifications, shifting from one unfinished task to checking the notifications. People may need to catch important calls, but app distractions are constant interruptions that are harder on young people than on adults. Both recognize that these interruptions hinder work and educational performance. AI algorithms will continue to learn people's habits and intentionally promote pings and triggers to their feeds to keep people on their phones. The social platform is catering to people's personal tastes, tempting many to eat everything it has to offer. It is important to master these devices rather than have them master us.

Another concern of social media is the rise of anxiety from the constant stream of news regularly presented to people. Humanity was created with limitations. We are not all-knowing and were not created to carry all the weight of the world. Haidt claims the young people's "mental health crisis is

8. Haidt, *Anxious Generation*, 126.

not because the world events suddenly got worse around 2012; it's because world events were suddenly being pumped into adolescents' brains through their phones, not as news stories but as social media posts in which other young people expressed their emotions about a collapsing world."[9] People were not created to carry the problems of the world. But now in real time, people can access many countries and watch real-time wars unfold. The internet allows people to hear and see all sorts of atrocities. When people's minds are constantly filled with the fallenness of the world, it can be overwhelming. It is important to remind people that God is in control. He cares about people and hope is found in him. Psalm 131 offers an excellent picture of care:

> O Lord, my heart is not proud, nor my eyes haughty;
> Nor do I involve myself in great matters,
> Or in things too difficult for me.
> Surely I have composed and quieted my soul;
> Like a weaned child *rests* against his mother,
> My soul is like a weaned child within me.
> O Israel, hope in the Lord
> From this time forth and forever.

It is good to ask questions when anxiety arises. Notice the psalmist says, "Nor do I involve myself in great matters, or in things too difficult for me." Ask yourself, am I involving myself in great matters that are too difficult for me? Maybe it is a moment to recognize that some news matters before us are not meant for us to carry. But we can ask God to help the situation and lay the problem at his throne and quiet our fears by resting in knowing that he will work all things out for our good and his glory for those who trust in him.

It is good to know that even the ancients dealt with the struggles of fear and anxiety. You are not alone if you are facing challenges with anxiety. Maybe you need to talk to someone about it. You can also engage with your community and renew your mind with God's word. Philippians 4:4–7 provides a practical method:

> Rejoice in the Lord always; again I will say, rejoice! Let your gentle *spirit* be known to all men. The Lord is near. Be anxious for nothing, but in everything by prayer and supplication with thanksgiving let your requests be made known to God. And the peace of God, which surpasses all comprehension, will guard your hearts and your minds in Christ Jesus.

9. Haidt, *Anxious Generation*, 39.

Instead of finding certain limited joy in social media, you can think of the Lord and his goodness. Take a walk outside and experience ten to twenty minutes of nature. Think upon the beauty of creation. Start a journal and offer a prayer to God. Ask him to help you use social media wisely. Journal your thanksgiving thoughts and look forward to the peace of God that surpasses all understanding. Be consistent in meeting with the Lord and praying to him.

CHATBOTS

Positive Aspects of Chatbots

The use of chatbots is on the rise. According to Pew Research, "34% of U.S. adults say they have used ChatGPT. That includes a 58% majority of adults under 30."[10] Chatbots are being leveraged to help individuals in businesses. Scott Lindsey, executive director for Logos Bible software, discusses bringing research into the twenty-first century with Wesley Huff on Huff's YouTube channel. Logos is the most widely used Bible software, and Lindsey says they are using AI with guardrails. This AI is not connected to the internet but rather is tied solely to the information in Logos. Logos has access to 300,000 books and is an excellent help to many who study the Bible. This is a great example of people using the tools to help people learn about God's word. In addition, businesses are leveraging their work utilizing AI. Keri Smith, senior vice president at HHHunt, discusses their HR bot on the Life in the Leadership Lane podcast with Bruce Waller.[11] Their bot, named Hunter, assists their team by providing quick access to answers. I also have friends who are developing bots to help their clients with quicker service. Chatbots, in this manner, are helping people in efficiency and productivity.

Negative Aspects of Chatbots

An important concern to keep in mind is the tendency to forget that chatbots are artificial intelligence; they are machines. Sometimes people can unintentionally fall into anthropomorphism, by which I mean giving machines human characteristics. These machines, to some degree, are

10. Sidoti and McClain, "34% of U.S. Adults," para. 1.

11. Waller, "Keri Smith."

imitating humanity; chatbots are a country of geniuses in a data center.[12] Examples of anthropomorphism emerge through human names and voices so that when people interact with them, the machines act as social agents. These things can make the chatbots more user-friendly, but people should always keep in mind that they are interacting with a computer. Machines can go awry: they can present harmful information and hallucinate, leading the chatbot to produce nonsensical or inaccurate outputs.[13]

Another concern arises from people turning to AI for friendships, especially among teens. "[AI] has opened a perplexing new frontier in modern friendship, with many teens turning to AI chatbots for academic help, entertainment, and even emotional support with few boundaries and protections."[14] Chatbots have no emotion or true care for humanity, and they are merely artificially mimicking a friendship:

> A 2024 Common Sense Media survey found that 70% of teens have used generative AI. Popular tools like ChatGPT, Character. AI, and Snapchat's My AI can mimic real conversations, and there is evidence that some of these bots are being used by socially isolated youth seeking companionship.[15]

These machines are drawing on all the accessible information they have and spitting it out when people ask them questions. "Experts warn chatbots are designed to prioritize engagement over user well-being. 'They are purposely programmed to be both user-affirming and agreeable because the creators want these kids to form strong attachments to them.'"[16] Sadly, ChatGPT played a role in a young person taking his life. The *New York Times* shared the story with the title "A Teen Was Suicidal, ChatGPT Was the Friend He Confided In." The *New York Times* claims in the article that "More people are turning to general-purpose chatbots for emotional support. At first, Adam Reine, 16, used ChatGPT for schoolwork, but then he started discussing plans to end his life."[17] What started out as a help to the young person ended in tragedy. There is a real danger for kids who seek friendship and advice from the machines.

12. Lydiate, "To 'GPT' or Not 'GPT.'"
13. IBM, "What Are AI Hallucinations?"
14. Andoh, "Many Teens Are Turning," para. 1.
15. Andoh, "Many Teens Are Turning," para. 19.
16. Andoh, "Many Teens Are Turning," para. 22.
17. Hill, "Teen Was Suicidal," subtitle.

The rise of attempting to help kids, autistic kids, and the elderly with chatbots is being tested today. In addition to online chatbots, companies are now developing toy chatbots. The testing of the chatbots made headlines with "AI-Powered Toys Caught Telling 5-Year-Olds How to Find Knives and Start Fires with Matches."[18] Another one they tested gave explicit advice on sexual activities. These toys are intended for kids ages three to twelve.

An added concern is the replacement of counselors and pastors with chatbots. There are a couple of reasons people are seeing a rise in counseling chatbots: low cost and accessibility.[19] The article "Exploring the Dangers of AI in Mental Healthcare" discusses counseling chatbots.[20] The author says, "New research from Stanford University shows that these tools can introduce biases and failures that could result in dangerous consequences."[21] Society should not be seeking counsel from a non-living machine. People should seek wise counsel, and the Scriptures encourage it. Proverbs 8:14 says counsel is given by God and from wisdom. And the following proverbs encourage seeking counsel from God's people:

- "Where there is no guidance, a people falls, but in an abundance of counselors there is safety" (Prov 11:14).
- "Listen to advice and accept instruction, that you may gain wisdom in the future" (Prov 19:20).
- "All Scripture is breathed out by God and profitable for teaching, for reproof, for correction, and for training in righteousness, that the man of God may be competent, equipped for every good work" (2 Tim 3:16–17).

When people are hurting and need counsel, human interaction is imperative. A machine cannot see the tears in an individual's eyes or notice the body language when someone is downcast. We are to help one another, pray for one another, and love one another.

People who would once have contacted a friend, church, or a pastor for counsel can now access online sites or download an app to ask spiritual questions. The article title reveals this new trend: "Meet Chatbot Jesus:

18. Landymore, "AI-Powered Toys."
19. Human-Centered Artificial Intelligence, "Exploring the Dangers of AI."
20. Human-Centered Artificial Intelligence, "Exploring the Dangers of AI."
21. Human-Centered Artificial Intelligence, "Exploring the Dangers of AI," para. 2.

Churches Tap AI to Save Souls—and Time." The author of the article relates that chatbots matter to these leaders advancing Jesus chatbots because

> AI is helping some churches stay relevant in the face of shrinking staff, empty pews and growing online audiences. But the practice raises new questions about who, or what, is guiding the flock.
> New AI-powered apps allow you to "text with Jesus" or "talk to the Bible," giving the impression you are communicating with a deity or angel.
> Other apps can create personalized prayers, let you confess your sins or offer religious advice on life's decisions.[22]

Recently, I attended a conference and met a young lady who expressed her desire to learn more about her Christian faith. She didn't have anyone to ask, so she turned to ChatGPT. She was excited about the things she was learning about her faith. I was able to encourage her to read her Bible, but this was where she felt most comfortable gaining insights about Christianity. Due to bias and hallucinations (discussed below), people should be cautious to solely rely on these apps and online sites connected to the open internet for information.

A further concern is chatbot hallucinations. These happen when the chatbot "perceives patterns or objects that are nonexistent or imperceptible to human observers, creating outputs that are nonsensical or altogether inaccurate."[23] In short, the chatbot provides incorrect information. For example, according to IBM news, these chatbots offered the following inaccurate information:

- Google's Bard chatbot incorrectly claimed that the James Webb Space Telescope had captured the world's first images of a planet outside our solar system.
- Microsoft's chat AI, Sydney, admitted to falling in love with users and spying on Bing employees.
- Meta pulled its Galactica LLM demo in 2022, after it provided users inaccurate information, sometimes rooted in prejudice.[24]

These hallucinations can cause confusion among people seeking accuracy in their search to find truthful answers. Moreover, there will also be the risk

22. Contreras and Isaac, "Meet Chatbot Jesus," para. 2.
23. IBM, "What Are AI Hallucinations?," para. 1.
24. IBM, "What Are AI Hallucinations?"

of bias within the chatbots. Who is behind the chatbot's development? Does the company have the chatbot connected to the internet, or is it developed in-house with only the company's information? It is imperative that people using chatbots are aware of the potential risks and are continually removing these threats.

STEWARDING AI TECHNOLOGY

Although there are many important questions to answer regarding stewarding technology, this section will focus on two: What is my purpose? And how should I use technology? Let's consider the first question. What is humanity's purpose? What is humanity designed or created to do? People were created to worship God. Augustine wrote, "Man is one of your creatures . . . you made us for yourself and our hearts find no peace until they rest in you."[25] Life's meaning will not be found in a machine but in God. Throughout this book, the authors have shared that God created man in the beginning, but man sinned, and it is only by turning back to God that we can steward technology well. You can turn to God by confessing your sin against God and receiving Christ as your Lord and Savior. People are longing in their hearts for love, peace, and happiness. But nothing, not social media nor chatbots, can satisfy the true longing in our hearts. We will not be liked enough, efficient enough, or productive enough. Getting approval from the world will always be fleeting. God alone gives us our meaning and our purpose in life. The purpose of life is to know God and glorify him. When we understand that, then we can use technology to explore his amazing universe and steward it well.

The second question builds on the first question: How should I use technology if knowing God and glorifying God are of first importance? What are the greatest commands of his to follow? Let's turn to an answer that will guide us, mentioned in Matt 22:36–40:

> A lawyer asked Jesus a question, testing Him, "Teacher, which is the great commandment in the Law?" And He said to him,"'You shall love the Lord your God with all your heart, and with all your soul, and with all your mind.' This is the great and foremost commandment. The second is like it, 'You shall love your neighbor as yourself.' On these two commandments depend the whole Law and the Prophets."

25. Augustine, *Confessions*, 21.

As Christians, we should use technology to glorify God and love our neighbor as ourselves. He should be our priority in everything we write on social media and in everything we create. Loving God is the beginning of the guardrails that will be helpful to society, because we should care about people as a natural result. The Bible provides principles for navigating the world of AI in social media and chatbots. Matthew 12:36 warns us: "But I tell you that every careless word that people speak, they shall give an accounting for it in the day of judgment." This Scripture reminds us that our words matter. Proverbs 18:21 tells us that "death and life are in the power of the tongue." What we write is an extension of the tongue, and we must be aware of how we interact with these computer platforms. Therefore, here are three questions that can guide the use of social media and chatbots when reading and posting information:

1. Is this true or false?
2. Does it build up or tear down?
3. Does it amplify or diminish Christ's gospel?[26]

In addition to the three questions, there are many things to remember to help establish guardrails for using social media and chatbots, but due to space, we will only emphasize three. Remember, you can master the technology, or it can master you. The best way to master something is to have a plan that provides guardrails to help stay on course to glorify God. Here are three things to remember:

1. Social media and chatbots can be used to glorify God, if we have guardrails.
2. Social media and chatbots are shaping us, and algorithms are trying to keep you online.
3. Social media and chatbots assist us, but they can't replace in-person community.

As Christians using AI technology, we should pursue being intentional. We can use social media and chatbots to glorify God, and we should move to the next step and ask some questions.

1. What are the goals of using AI?

26. Henslee, "Ways to Harness Social Media."

2. What are the positives and what are the negative aspects of using AI technology?
3. Who is behind the chatbot?
4. Where is the information accessing its resources?
5. Is it connected to the internet, or is it an in-house chatbot?
6. How is it helpful to me in an ethical way?
7. Are there ways it can leverage my work in my job without losing the human connection?

You may have different questions to get you started, and that is good. Being intentional is considering the long-term goals and costs of your endeavor. Proverbs 24:27 says, "Prepare your work outside, and make it ready for yourself in the field; Afterwards, then, build your house." To be intentional is to prepare. Parents can help prepare their teens by being involved with their teens' smartphones and online activities. Show them examples of good ways to interact with social media and chatbots. When parents and grandparents speak into the lives of their children, they may think they're not listening, but my experience tells me they are listening. I recall my mom often reminding me when things seemed hard or confusing that God had a plan and was working it out for good. And I still carry the words in my head that my Grandma Fults once wrote in her journal, "The only ones you try to get even with are the ones that do you good."

Furthermore, be involved in your church community and read the Bible daily to give you the mind of Christ. The church is a group of imperfect people saved by grace. There will be times of joy and heartache, but if believers are willing to walk by the Spirit and grow in the fruit of the Spirit, then they can experience true community. Sometimes you may encounter tough things in the church, but you will also encounter tough things in the world. The Bible provides principles we can follow to enjoy community and to steward the emerging AI world we are encountering.

CONCLUSION

Although there are numerous positive and negative aspects of AI, social media, and chatbots, this chapter has focused on some of the most common ones. The argument is that the church has the answers to pave the way for using AI technology well. Even if a person is not a Christian, the principles of God's word are universal and can help a society flourish as they use technology to love their neighbor as themselves. Remember to start thinking about a plan for how to interact with AI chatbots. Ask yourself good questions about the technology and recognize the positive and negative aspects, so that you can help them steward technology well. It is important to remember that technology is not meant to replace human connections, but humans can leverage technology to encourage a society.

BIBLIOGRAPHY

Andoh, Efua. "Many Teens Are Turning to AI Chatbots for Friendship and Emotional Support." *Monitor on Psychology* 56.7 (2025) 51. https://www.apa.org/monitor/2025/10/technology-youth-friendships.

Augustine. *Confessions*. Translated by R. S. Pine-Coffin. London: Penguin, 1961.

Coeckelbergh, Mark. *AI Ethics*. Cambridge, MA: MIT Press, 2020.

Contreras, Russell, and Isaac Avilucea. "Meet Chatbot Jesus: How Churches Are Using AI to Save Souls." Axios, Nov. 12, 2025. https://www.axios.com/2025/11/12/christian-ai-chatbot-jesus-god-satan-churches.

Haidt, Jonathan. *The Anxious Generation*. New York: Penguin, 2024.

Henslee, Matt. "3 Ways to Harness Social Media to the Glory of God." Lifeway Research, Jan. 27, 2020. https://research.lifeway.com/2020/01/27/3-ways-to-harness-social-media-to-the-glory-of-god/.

Hill, Kashmir. "A Teen Was Suicidal. ChatGPT Was the Friend He Confided In." *New York Times*, Aug. 26, 2025. https://www.nytimes.com/2025/08/26/technology/chatgpt-openai-suicide.html.

Human-Centered Artificial Intelligence. "Exploring the Dangers of AI in Mental Health Care." Stanford University. https://hai.stanford.edu/news/exploring-the-dangers-of-ai-in-mental-health-care.

IBM. "What Are AI Hallucinations?" https://www.ibm.com/think/topics/ai-hallucinations.

Landymore, Frank. "AI-Powered Toys Caught Telling 5-Year-Olds How to Find Knives and Start Fires With Matches." *Futurism*, Nov. 13, 2025. https://futurism.com/artificial-intelligence/ai-toys-danger.

Lax, Allison. "Parents Frantic to Shield Teens from 'Addictive' Screen Time Are Turning to 'Detox' Camps and Even Other Tech." New York Post, Nov. 18, 2025. https://nypost.com/2025/11/17/lifestyle/frantic-parents-turn-to-detox-camps-for-tech-obsessed-kids/.

Lydiate, Troy. "To 'GPT' or not 'GPT' with Gretchen Huizinga." *The AC Podcast*, episode 572, Oct. 24, 2025. https://podcasts.apple.com/ca/podcast/to-gpt-or-not-gpt-with-gretchen-huizinga/id732235712?i=1000733357746.

Reinke, Tony. *God, Technology, and the Christian Life*. Wheaton, IL: Crossway, 2022.

Sidoti, Olivia, and Colleen McClain. "34% of U.S. Adults Have Used ChatGPT, About Double the Share in 2023." Pew Research Center, June 25, 2025. https://www.pewresearch.org/short-reads/2025/06/25/34-of-us-adults-have-used-chatgpt-about-double-the-share-in-2023/.

Waller, Bruce. "Keri Smith, Senior Vice President Human Resources on Life in the Leadership Lane: Trust Builder." Nov. 15, 2025. YouTube video, 35:14. https://www.youtube.com/watch?v=cKvcQz6JriY.

Final Thoughts

Deanna Huff, PhD

Stand by the ways and see and ask for the ancient paths,

Where the good way is, and walk in it;

And you will find rest for your souls.

—Jeremiah 6:16

As you have read, the world of AI is here. How will we interact with it? On the one hand, some people will offer a tech-dystopian, pessimistic view, calling for everyone to live in a city free of technology. On the other hand, some secular humanists and posthumanists will offer a utopian view, calling for people to merge with technology to evolve into a new species. But I tend to agree with Tony Reinke on another way forward. He says, "I land in the mix, not a dystopian and not a utopian, but a Bible-believing creationist."[1] The path forward is to build guardrails from the Bible to steward AI.

God has provided principles through the Scriptures that help us promote good even in a fallen world. He has allowed humanity to explore his amazing universe. Stewardship is God's delegation to man to rule and use creation's resources to flourish in society. Stewarding AI should be glorifying to God. Stewardship is using God's wisdom.

In the book, the authors have offered ways forward for using the incredible technology effectively and for revealing its dangers. Throughout

1. Reinke, *God, Technology, and Christian Life*, 25.

the last one hundred years, many people have witnessed the vast changes in technology. Communication has shifted from the talking telegraph to the smartphone; travel has shifted from horse carriage to the automobile to flight; healthcare has advanced from penicillin to gene editing; and domestic life has received refrigerators, washing machines, color TVs, microwaves, and so much more. Many of these technological advancements have both positive and negative aspects. The future of an AI world will also hold both positive and negative aspects.

We could not mention every advancement in AI technology, but even if we could, the principles for stewarding AI would remain the same. The main thrust of the book is to say that God has provided a way forward in handling AI, and it starts with knowing him and using technology for his glory. Secondly, we are to love our neighbor as ourselves. Third, the principles that guide our ethical actions are grounded in those two truths and are found in the Bible. Christians have the opportunity to steward technology well and influence society in a way that recognizes the good way God has provided for us. Let's go steward AI well.

BIBLIOGRAPHY

Reinke, Tony. *God, Technology, and the Christian Life.* Wheaton, IL: Crossway, 2022.

www.ingramcontent.com/pod-product-compliance
Lightning Source LLC
LaVergne TN
LVHW020627100826
845148LV00012B/2087